HOW MINORITY STUDENTS
EXPERIENCE COLLEGE

HOW MINORITY STUDENTS EXPERIENCE COLLEGE

Implications for Planning and Policy

Lemuel W. Watson
Melvin C. Terrell
Doris J. Wright
Fred A. Bonner II

Michael J. Cuyjet
James A. Gold
Donna E. Rudy
Dawn R. Person

Sty/us

STERLING, VIRGINIA

Published in 2002 by

Stylus Publishing, LLC
22883 Quicksilver Drive
Sterling, Virginia 20166

Library of Congress Cataloging-in-Publication Data

How minority students experience college : the implications for plannir and policy / Lemuel W. Watson ... [et al.].– 1st ed.
   p. cm.
Includes bibliographical references and index.
  ISBN 1-57922-048-7 (alk. paper) – ISBN 1-57922-049-5 (pbk. : alk. paper)
1. Minority college students–United States. 2. Minorities–Education (Higher)–United States. 3. Multicultural education–United States. I. Watson, Lemuel W. (Lemuel Warren)
  LC3727 .H66 2002
  378.1'9829–dc21
             2001057551

First edition, 2002
ISBN, hard cover: 1-57922-048-7
     paperback: 1-57922-049-5

Printed in the United States of America

All first editions printed on acid-free paper.

This book is dedicated to all of our ancestors—

   —*who had a vision for their children, grandchildren, and great grandchildren*

   —*who fought and died for our rights to obtain an equal education*

   —*who continue to live through us in our efforts to pursue and protect life, liberty, and freedom.*

CONTENTS

PREFACE

The notions of cultural differences and similarities continue to be topics of major concern for educators, humanitarians, and politicians. Books, movies, and documentaries inform us of the advantages and disadvantages for any society choosing to divide and discriminate among its citizens on the basis of race and ethnicity. Enormous amounts of energy and resources have been expended on multicultural initiatives in higher education and industry in the name of creating civility and comfort in the workplace. This has generated a number of questions, such as: What are we truly trying to accomplish with an integrated society? What do we really mean, in the short term and long term, when we speak of a multicultural campus community? Do we have a vision of what a multicultural campus should look like, and how do we operationalize a campus to be welcoming to all students while providing a safe zone for free and civil debate to spark development for responsive citizens?

After three decades of integration and multicultural initiatives, can we truly say that our ongoing multicultural efforts have provided a better education for all students? Are minority students and majority students reaping similar benefits for their efforts in colleges, specifically in predominantly White colleges? Do colleges and their agents know how to design a campus that is welcoming to all students? Are our professional and traditional theories appropriate and adaptable for our students' needs and issues? These are pivotal points to consider if we are to respond with a sound ethical and moral voice to discover the answers through this discourse.

The pathway to providing a quality education for all students while recognizing the diversity they bring to the academic setting is not a simple one. In fact, it takes a concerted effort and a sincere commitment by all involved for any institution to realize its multicultural vision. The institutions identified in this book seem to be heading in positive directions, becoming campuses that embrace cultural differences and welcome opportunities to openly discuss controversial issues, thus supporting and challenging their students' development.

The voices of students of color are the cornerstone of this book. We have gone to great lengths to preserve and present their voices, to share the most moving experiences of their college lives. This book also confirms the theory advanced in previously published works on college students' experiences: To succeed in college, students from all racial groups need to experience a variety of challenges in and out of the classroom while finding something or someone to connect them to their respective campus environments.

Purpose

The institutions highlighted in this book serve as models for higher education. The data obtained are from students who volunteered to share their personal stories of pain and happiness engendered by their college experiences. Administrators will be able to identify numerous issues impacting minority student populations and be afforded the opportunity to investigate the changes needed to enhance learning and development. The information on which this book is based includes a yearlong investigation of seven colleges and many minority students.

Using qualitative techniques such as focus groups, structured interviews, and document analysis, the team of researchers collected data about the experiences of minority students at small, private, predominantly White institutions. Our goal was to identify important commonalties among institutions with predominantly White students that have maintained high minority-student retention rates. It is our hope that the results of this research will fill the gaps in our knowledge of minority students' educational experiences.

This book is not intended to serve as a "how-to" manual for making a college campus multicultural. It is simply a guide designed to take the reader on a journey through a land of diverse ideas and voices, with the overarching mission of providing the traveler with insight on current and professional practices related to multiculturalism. The traveler might be an administrator, faculty member, or student affairs professional. This book takes a complex, emotional, personal, and controversial issue—multiculturalism—and attempts to demystify it by providing the reader with what is perhaps the most important and overlooked perspective, that of the students.

Audience

The primary audience for this book is comprised of practitioners and leaders in higher education, particularly in the field of student affairs administration. Practitioners in programs targeting specific campus-based student groups such as women, returning adults, African Americans, Hispanics, Asians, American Indians, and mixed-race students will find this material especially applicable to their work. Presidents, academic affairs professionals, student affairs professionals, and faculty interested in helping minority students should find this book helpful and enlightening. Additionally, anyone who has been frustrated by the cultural tensions often present on college campuses will find this book beneficial. This book is for you if you have ever questioned your sensitivity to or understanding of individual differences. Appreciation of differences is not automatic. Most of us do not wish to be viewed as bigots or as individuals harboring prejudice, but we simply lack the confidence and expertise to deal with issues of diversity. Thus, most of us approach diversity and multiculturalism with apprehension due to our desire not to be offensive.

This book was mainly intended for academic and student affairs administrators who work with college and university students. It will also assist faculty members who are unsure about ways to nurture and support minority students' educational experiences. Equally important, this book will bring administrators, faculty members, and other professionals face to face with their biases by helping them to identify personal deficits that hinder development of awareness, sensitivity, knowledge, and skills required to provide a campus environment that is welcoming to minority students. Professors in graduate programs will find this book a valuable source of information as well as a supplementary textbook.

Scope and Treatment

This book provides a cross-cultural perspective to assist educators and professionals in moving their institutions toward the ideal of a well-adapted multicultural campus. The students' voices in this book represent African American or Black, Asian American, Hispanic (Chicano, Latino, Mexican), Native American or American Indian, and biracial and other students who have self-identified as minority students. Sometimes we refer to minority students as "students of color"; our intentions are not to offend, but to identify a term that would be understood regardless of the political climate. The term *minority* does not imply that these students are fewer in number than the majority students. In fact, on one campus, the number of minority students almost equals that of majority students.

We are sure other important issues and paradigms may have been overlooked; yet, we believe the information cited here regarding race, student development, data techniques, and assessment provides a valuable perspective often ignored by fellow researchers. Rarely does the literature and research highlight for the reader the concerns of students in their own words.

This book does not set out to create any elaborate framework for institutional implementation; however, we do offer suggestions. Institutions and humans are far too diverse to implement cookie-cutter approaches. What we present in this book are the students' concerns so that they may be used to guide practice. Where necessary, to set the stage and give supporting documentation to the reader, we do not hesitate to follow the naturalistic approach of informing the reader of issues or concerns primarily through our own contextual lenses.

Overview of the Contents

This book has seven chapters. Within these pages we define terms, outline our rationale for the study, and enumerate upon the research questions which have guided us in our quest to discover minority students' college experiences. Chapter 1 is a brief prologue about the multicultural institution. Appropriate literature is provided for support. Chapter 2 profiles the seven institutions included in the study so that readers can become acquainted with them. Chapter 3 describes how the institutions were selected and discusses the questions guiding the study and methodology. The chapter includes a brief overview and introductory section and a detailed conceptually clustered matrix of the findings from the seven institutions. This introduction sets the stage for the next three chapters.

Chapters 4 through 6 present students' perceptions of their educational experiences. Supporting literature, a rationale, a list of recommendations, and a set of implications are included. Chapter 4 gives the reader a powerful example of the students' perceptions about the reality of campus culture. Chapter 5 relates to how the lack of multicultural awareness and practices affect their college experiences. Chapter 6 portrays the experiences that multicultural students must face to become successful in predominantly White institutions. In all, these chapters present issues related to coping, involvement, identity, and educational outcomes.

Chapter 7 provides a discussion about the findings and gives the reader suggestions and concluding thoughts about the future of minority students in higher education.

Acknowledgments

The journey to fruition for this book is the result of supporters and contributors from many institutions. I would like to acknowledge my parents, Ethel Lee and Cleveland (deceased) Terrell, for instilling in me the importance of education, perseverance, and the hard work necessary to achieve my personal and professional goals. For taking this particular project to its conclusion, I acknowledge my colleague, Dr. Lemuel W. Watson, Associate Professor of Higher Education at Clemson University. We met at a NASPA conference in Boston and from that day forward have maintained a relationship as colleagues and close friends. I thank the authors for their contribution to this project. Dr. Salme Harje Steinberg, President of Northeastern Illinois University, has allowed me to grow as a college administrator and researcher in the area of diversity and college student culture. Dr. Doris W. Wright, a close colleague and friend, has provided the encouragement without which many of my writings would not exist and has given me the guidance that has enabled me to make a contribution to the student affairs profession. Special recognition goes to the numerous mentees who I have counseled and advised during my twenty-five-year career for giving me the opportunity to assist them in the development of their academic and career goals and, in turn, allowing me to learn from them. Hopefully, I have made as much a contribution to their professional development as they have to mine. Mrs. Wilma J. Sutton is a long-term mentor who has always encouraged me to publish and to encourage other talented writers. I am indebted also to my student affairs staff at Northeastern Illinois University for their advice and counsel over the years. Dean Murrell Duster, a colleague and friend, has always encouraged me and supported my professional development. My sincere gratitude to Dr. Fred

Bonner of the University of Texas at San Antonio for his extensive and intensive editing of this manuscript, and to Mr. Tramayne Whitney, a mentee who has supported and encouraged me throughout this project. For her initial involvement in this project, I acknowledge Ms. A. Alyce Claerbaut. She assisted with the logistics and coordinated the Multicultural Study Team. I would also like to recognize Dr. Harry Schuler, who journeyed to one college with me and assisted in the interview process; and Gayl J. Johnson, my project assistant, for her proofreading and editing skills as they applied to this book. I am also grateful to the entire research team (Michael J. Cuyjet, James A. Gold, Donna E. Rudy, and Dawn R. Person) for their time and energy to assist in completing this project.

Melvin C. Terrell, Ph.D.

Fred A. Bonner II is assistant professor of the Adult and Higher Education program at the University of Texas at San Antonio. He received his B.A. degree (1991) in chemistry from the University of North Texas, his M.S.Ed. degree (1994) in curriculum and instruction from Baylor University, and his Ed.D. degree (1997) in higher education administration and college teaching from the University of Arkansas–Fayetteville. He was the recipient of the American Association for Higher Education Black Caucus Dissertation Award and the Educational Leadership, Counseling, and Foundation's Dissertation of the Year Award from the University of Arkansas College of Education. He currently serves as assistant editor to the *National Association of Student Affairs Professionals Journal,* and is completing a research fellowship with the Yale University Psychology Department (PACE Center), focusing on issues that impact academically gifted African American male college students.

Michael J. Cuyjet is associate dean of the Graduate School at the University of Louisville as well as an associate professor in the Department of Educational and Counseling Psychology, where he is also the coordinator of the College Student Personnel program for master's and doctoral students. He earned a B.S. degree (1969) in speech communications from Bradley University, an M.S.Ed. degree (1973) in counseling and an Ed.D. degree (1983) in counselor education from Northern Illinois University, where he served as a student affairs practitioner for more than fourteen years. Prior to his current appointments, he served as a student affairs administrator and an affiliate assistant professor at the University of Maryland at College Park.

Cuyjet has published nineteen journal articles or book chapters, has edited two monographs, and made over thirty presentations at national and regional student affairs and student activities conferences or conventions. His most recent book is *Helping African American Men Succeed in College*. He currently serves on the editorial board of the *National Association of Student Affairs Professionals Journal*. Cuyjet has been an active leader in several national professional organizations, most recently in the American College Personnel Association (ACPA). He has served on the ACPA Educational Leadership Foundation Board of Trustees, the Directorate Body of Commission XII (Preparation Program Faculty), the Directorate Body of Commission I (Administrative Leadership), the Directorate Body of Commission IV (Students, Their Activities and Their Community), and the Executive Director Screening Committee; he also has served as the 1988 National Convention Featured Speakers chair and the faculty liaison to the 2000 National Convention Planning Committee, as a member of the ACPA Executive Council, and as chair-elect, chair, past chair, and historian of the ACPA Standing Committee on Multicultural Affairs. He has received ACPA's Annuit Coeptis Award twice, once as an emerging professional in 1981 and again as a senior professional in 1998.

James A. Gold is professor emeritus of the Educational Foundations and College Student Personnel Administration program at State University of New York at Buffalo State. Dr. Gold, having retired from full-time teaching in Fall 2000, continues to teach graduate courses in college student personnel administration, counseling, and student development theory. He taught full time for a decade after serving thirteen years as vice president for student affairs at the same institution. He also served in a number of administrative, teaching, and counseling roles at the University of Rhode Island and Pennsylvania State University. He edited the *NASPA Monograph Series,* and his own writings focus upon student affairs administration, career development, transformational leadership, and counseling. His doctorate degree is from Pennsylvania State University.

Dawn R. Person is professor of counseling and student development in higher education at California State University at Long Beach. She coordinates a master's degree program that emphasizes student development/affairs in higher education. Prior to her decade of college teaching, she served as a counselor, advisor, and administrator in student affairs, coordinating programs and services in support of students of color, international students, first-year students, and student athletes. Dr. Person serves as a consultant to college and universities on multicultural issues, student retention, and organization change.

Dr. Person currently is an internal evaluator for a grant focusing on standards-based teacher education at Cerritos College and a Howard Hughes Medical Institute Access to Science grant at California State University at Long Beach. She recently completed a four-year project as consultant for the reorganization of the undergraduate student affairs division of Columbia University. She was the principal investigator of a longitudinal study on Black and Hispanic student retention in math, science, and engineering funded by the William Penn Foundation.

Dr. Person has published articles and book chapters on student retention, women and student athletes of color, and success factors influencing the retention of students of color in higher education. She serves as a reviewer for two higher education journals and on an editorial board. Among her many honors and awards, Dr. Person received the College of Education Most Valuable Professor in 1999.

Donna Rudy is vice president for student services at Kellogg Community College. Previously she held administrative positions at Northeastern Illinois University and Elgin Community College. Her undergraduate degree is from the University of Illinois, her master's degree is from Northern Illinois University, and her Ph.D. is from Loyola University of Chicago. She has coauthored a number of articles and chapters with Dr. Melvin C. Terrell about emerging issues in the student affairs profession.

Melvin C. Terrell currently serves as the vice president for student affairs and professor of Counselor Education at Northeastern Illinois University. He received his B.S. degree in history from Chicago State University (1971), his M.Ed. degree (1974) in student personnel work in higher education from Loyola University of Chicago, and his Ph.D. (1978) in higher education administration from Southern Illinois University in Carbondale. He has also done postdoctoral work at Harvard University and the University of Virginia. Noted for his expertise in the area of student affairs/ minority student issues, Dr. Terrell has coauthored and edited numerous books and articles. Currently he serves as editor of the *National Association of Student Affairs Professionals Journal.* He has served as a guest editor and editorial board member for the *Illinois Committee on Black Concerns in Higher Education Journal, Journal of College Student Development, Journal of the National Council of Education Opportunity Associations, National Association of Student Personnel Administrators Journal,* and the University of Wisconsin System, American Ethnic Studies Coordinating Committee, Urban Corridor Consortium Public Policy Series, Volumes 1, 2, and 3.

Dr. Terrell has held leadership positions in several professional organizations. He is the immediate past president of the National Association of Student Affairs Professionals (NASAP). He serves as a member of the National Association of Student Personnel Administrators' (NASPA) National Board of the Health Education and Leadership program and was the national coordinator of NASPA's Minority Undergraduate Fellows program. Dr. Terrell is the past chair of the Illinois Committee on Black Concerns in Higher Education (ICBCHE) and has served as caucus chair of the American Association of Higher Education (AAHE)'s Black Caucus. In recognition of his leadership potential, the American Council on Education awarded Dr. Terrell a fellowship (class of 1993–1994) to serve at Florida State University. Dr. Terrell has the distinction of being the first minority to receive the NASPA Region IV—East Scott Goodnight Award for outstanding service as a dean. NASPA also bestowed on him its 2001 Exemplary Service Award for the minority mentorship program he instituted at Northeastern Illinois University. He has also been listed in *Who's Who in Black America* since 1988.

Lemuel W. Watson is associate professor of higher education in the Educational Leadership Area at Clemson University. He received his B.S. degree in business from the University of South Carolina, his M.A. degree from Ball State University, and his doctorate of education degree from Indiana University. He is a certified training consultant and systems engineer. His career spans various divisions in higher education, faculty, and administration, and he has numerous experiences in two-year and four-year institutions, both public and private. His research agenda surrounds issues of educational outcomes; faculty development issues; and social and political issues that affect schools, community, and families with regard to advancement in a capitalist society.

He is also senior research fellow for the Charles Hamilton Houston Center at Clemson University, and a research fellow with the Institute for Southern Studies at the University of South Carolina. Dr. Watson has been working on frameworks and paradigms to assist in the educational process and outcomes of minority students in both the K–12 and postsecondary schools and colleges. He provides workshops, seminars, and consultation on issues related to educational outcomes, especially for minority students. He also serves on the research team for the "Call Me Mister Program" to recruit 600 African American male elementary teachers in South Carolina. In addition, he has expertise in building quality graduate programs in student affairs and higher education. He has written articles and chapters, and has coedited a number of monographs. He has given over fifty presentations at local, state, national, and international conferences. Dr. Watson serves on the board of six journals and is a reviewer, assistant, and associate editor. He is an active member in the American Association of Higher Education (AAHE) American Educational Research Association (AERA), Association for the Student of Higher Education (ASHE), National Association of Student Affairs Professionals (NASAP), American College Personnel Association (ACPA), and National Association of Student Personnel Administrators (NASPA).

Doris J. Wright is currently associate professor of Counseling and Educational Psychology and coordinator of the College Student Personnel program at Kansas State University in Manhattan, Kansas. Dr. Wright has more than twenty-five years of teaching and counseling experience helping colleges to develop programs that promote the achievement of underrepresented groups, including multicultural and female students. Doris has given more than fifty presentations and written more than twenty-five articles, papers, and chapters. She has edited or coauthored three books including the well-cited, *Responding to the Needs of Today's Minority Students. New Directions in Student Services (1987),* where she outlined a blueprint for multicultural services. In 1988, she and coauthor Melvin C. Terrell edited the monograph, *From Survival to Success: Promoting Minority Student Retention,* a text that directed the future of multicultural student affairs. Dr. Wright received her B.S. degree in psychology and her M.S. degree in education from Kansas State University. She holds a Ph.D. in counseling psychology from the University of Nebraska at Lincoln. She participates in the American Psychological Association (APA), American College Personnel Association (ACPA), National Association of Student Personnel Administrators (NASPA), and American Association of Higher Education (AAHE).

HOW MINORITY STUDENTS
EXPERIENCE COLLEGE

INTRODUCTION

Institutions in the twentieth century have had to deal with difficult challenges regarding multiculturalism. In fact, mission statements for institutions of higher education continue to be ambiguous in their definitions, leaving in question the institutions' true identities and roles in this age of adaptation to technology, demographics, and societal change. Most mission statements emphasize students, teaching, community service, and diversity as priority issues, yet these values do not appear reflective of their practice (Watson, 1998).

The university, historically, has placed multiculturalism at its core. For example, Newman (1901) reports that

> Our student has determined on entering himself as a disciple of Theophrastus, a teacher of marvelous popularity, who has brought together two thousand pupils from all parts of the

world. He himself is of Lesbos; for masters, as well as students, come hither from all regions of the earth, as befits a University. It is the range of territory, which the notion of a University implies, which furnished both the quantity of the one, and the quality of the other. Anaxagoras was from Ionia, Carneades from Africa, Zeno from Cyprus, Protagoras from Thrace, and Gorgias from Sicily. (p. 60)

An egalitarian ethos appears to encapsulate Newman's concept of the university. To bring various cultures from different regions of the world was viewed as a befitting ideal for Athens and for the concept of the university: "There was a brotherhood and a citizenship of mind" (p. 60). This notion of the university best describes an institution committed to quality education for all involved. The United States system of higher education has developed a curriculum resembling this ideal.

Today, institutions of higher education are coming to the realization that they are inadequately prepared to understand the learning and developmental needs of racial, cultural, and linguistic minorities. College students require institutions of higher education to address the pluralistic nature of American society with its multifaceted, institutional fabric. Colleges in the twenty-first century must not only educate racial and cultural minorities to their value within their particular microcultural enclaves, but they must also enlighten White people to the value and richness of racial and cultural diversity in society at large. This task is a formidable one, and not to be taken lightly. Comprehensive reviews of studies on multicultural education demonstrate that for the past decade, demographics have been shifting toward an increase in the minority population throughout the United States (Jones, 2001). As the population of our country rapidly becomes more diverse, faculty and administrators in higher education must be prepared to meet students' educational and cultural needs on a broader basis than ever before.

Discovering how best to educate racial and cultural minorities while expanding White students' awareness of multiculturalism are challenges facing colleges and universities. Colleges have initiated and developed a plethora of innovative programs, services, and environments all designed to help minority students succeed in college; however, they have spent far less time attending to the multicultural aspects of college life. Although American colleges and universities reflect upon more than thirty years of programming aimed at minority student retention, the success of their intentional efforts toward multiculturalism and acceptance of diversity is minimal at best.

In considering the themes and initiatives of institutions of higher education, and the voices of their students as presented in this book, perhaps a clearer vision might emerge for institutions and their agents in their quest to create environments that are affirming to all students. For example, one could use a garden as the metaphor for a college campus and gardeners for the institution's agents. To reap benefits from a garden, the gardener must analyze the soil content and calculate the amount of nutrients necessary to nourish the crops; determine the number of sun hours versus shade hours; configure the layout of the garden based on each plants' height and growth period; and monitor moisture of the soil and irrigate as needed. By so doing, the gardener will promote the optimum development of each plant.

More important, to maintain a bountiful garden, weeds need constant picking and crops need constant attention to remain healthy. Some crops may need to be moved or protected during the winter months to ensure their survival; however, the vision that all are equally important and that together they make the garden a beautiful place continues to provide the gardener with a comprehensive mental framework. The higher education practitioner should also have a vision and not carelessly move from one initiative to another in the name of multiculturalism. Institutions must develop a vision and constantly assess the individual students and student subgroups, thus developing dynamic campus learning environments.

Utilizing qualitative techniques such as focus groups, structured interviews, and document analysis, the research team collected an array of data about the experiences of minority students at small, predominantly White liberal arts institutions. Our goal was to ascertain the most significant commonalties among institutions with predominantly White student populations that have maintained high retention rates for minority students. It is our hope that the results of this research will fill many existing gaps in current knowledge of minority students' experiences in these educational settings.

The multicultural colleges highlighted in this book serve as models for higher education. The students whose voices provided this data bestowed upon scholars and educators the opportunity for meaningful dialogue concerning their college experiences. Administrators will discover some changes that they must consider to enhance minority student learning and support for these students' personal growth. Institutions will obtain needed information to redefine their campus environments to fit an evolving, pluralistic college community.

With a commitment to multiculturalism as a precursor to change, this book is dedicated to characterizing the relationship between students of color and their respective institutions. The purpose of this investigation is to examine those postsecondary institutions that have had success in the development and marketing of multicultural experiences for students of color outside of the classroom. The specific aim of this research is twofold: (1) to characterize the range of students' out-of-classroom learning experiences, and (2) to identify institutional factors that promote their out-of-classroom learning and personal development. To that end, the investigative team sought to answer the following questions.

1. How do undergraduate students of color experience out-of-classroom learning? How do they characterize such experiences?

2. How does racial identity influence students of color and their out-of-classroom learning?

3. How does campus institutional climate influence the out-of-classroom learning for students of color?

Significance of Research

This current research extends the pioneering work of Kuh and associates (1991) and enhances the literature concerning multi-culturalism within higher education in four distinct ways.

1. Expands the understanding about minorities' out-of-classroom learning experiences and their personal development by emphasizing noncognitive success measures
2. Utilizes the advantages of qualitative research to record minority student's own voices in ways quantitative research cannot do
3. Offers innovations as to how culture-specific and multicultural programs should occur within academic and student affairs
4. Determines the means by which students of color perceive their place in the environment of predominantly White colleges and the means by which they adjust to the culture of these institutions

The beauty and challenge of this investigation was to answer these questions from a viewpoint not well understood in behavior research—through the eyes of the students themselves.

I
DEFINING MULTICULTURALISM

All educational institutions are charged with the creation and maintenance of a multicultural environment. Traditionally, the emphasis in higher education has been on maintaining institutional traditions and practices while reflecting the prevailing values and attitudes of society at large (Cheatham, 1991). The result of such emphasis can mean that individuals from underrepresented groups are encouraged to adapt to the existing, often inhospitable environment of the majority culture on college campuses (Stage and Manning, 1992). Although researchers have identified academic persistence factors, colleges remain uncertain of the noncognitive factors and out-of-classroom learning experiences that best promote learning for students of color.

Activity and social life outside of the classroom is a different matter, however. On predominantly White campuses, many minority students experience a climate of widespread distrust and victimization. A large number of White students believe that students of color receive special privileges such as lower admission standards, compensatory education, support programs, scholarships, and employment opportunities not afforded to them. These "special programs" have been the subject of much discussion and debate. Conservatives believe these initiatives constitute reverse discrimination. Indeed, court rulings (*University of Texas v. Hopwood*) and state legislation (e.g., Proposition 209 in California) have effectively eradicated or dismantled college affirmative action and special admissions programs in some regions of the country, claiming that Whites are being discriminated against when they are denied eligibility to participate in such programs and services.

Tierney (1992) suggested that the approaches used to foster the academic and social integration of underrepresented college students might be misdirected. The anthropological theory behind such efforts often involves the initiation of youths into their own culture, which precludes the possibility of failure and is akin to a rite of passage. Yet, this situation differs drastically from the one existing on most college campuses today where the prevailing culture may be different from the culture in which many minority students were raised. Boyer (1990) affirmed that a true campus community is multifaceted in terms of institutional characteristics and responsibilities. Among other attributes, a campus is to be a caring community, "a place where the well-being of each member is sensitively considered" (p. 47); an open community, "a place where freedom of expression is uncompromisingly protected and where civility is powerfully affirmed" (p. 17); and a just community, "a place where the sacredness of each person is honored and where diversity is aggressively pursued" (p. 25).

To foster the success of these efforts toward diversity and multiculturalism, institutions should ask of their campuses such questions as: Is the college really prepared to educate an increasingly diverse population? To what extent is the campus environment suitable for underrepresented students? Are the college's curricula, instructional practices, text materials, and styles of teaching appropriate for these students? As individual educators and administrators, what role should each of us play in the progressive changes for these issues? The discussions and resolutions of these questions are essential if institutions of higher education expect to fully realize their mission of quality and diversity in an educational and societal context.

In this chapter we discuss the meaning of multicultural colleges. A brief presentation of some of the issues surrounding multiculturalism, explored to set the context for remaining the chapters, follows.

Kuh and associates (1991) and other researchers have only tangentially addressed the needs of an ever-increasing minority student population. Critical questions raised, but not fully answered, include:

- How can colleges and universities accommodate the traditions and values of different groups and foster interactive multiculturalism?

- What organizational structures and support exist for different kinds of students to establish a sense of belonging?

- What strategies can be developed to synthesize intellectual, moral, social, and emotional issues and concerns across racial, ethnic, and other boundaries?

The challenge to institutions of higher education is to discover ways to shape the campus environment by encouraging minority student involvement and learning without singling them out as being different.

The first step in moving toward a multicultural organization is to understand the key terms and concepts relevant to the development of a multicultural campus environment. Borrowing a definition from the Association of Multicultural Counseling and Development, the term *multicultural* concerns those factors that focus on race, ethnicity, and culture (cited in Ivey, Ivey, and Simek-Morgan, 1997, pp. 32–33). *Multiculturalism* is viewed as the process of increasing awareness of and knowledge about human diversity in ways that are translated into respectful human interactions and effective interconnections (D'Andrea and Daniels, 1995).

Multiculturalism is seen as an action or set of interactions that intentionally promotes respect for human difference and positive, meaningful relations. Such interactions are based on, a fundamental belief that race and ethnic and cultural differences are valuable and should be included in a college's programs, curricula, and services.

Therefore, multiculturalism is a state of being in which humans feel comfortable in their communication with people from any culture, in any situation, because they desire to learn about others and are empathic in their quest. Accordingly, a "multicultural organization is one that is genuinely committed to diverse representation of its membership; is sensitive to maintaining an open, supportive and responsive environment; is working toward and purposefully including elements of diverse cultures in its ongoing operations; and . . . [i]s authentic in its response to issues confronting it" (Strong, 1986, as quoted in Barr and Strong, 1988, p. 85).

Cross (1991) states that institutions of higher education pass through three developmental stages regarding diversity. The challenge of making an institutional climate a multicultural environment requires that institutions move from maintaining a benign tolerance of campus segregation (cultural diversity) to designing campus environments that value multiculturalism. Within the first stage is a single culture that excludes students of color and other minorities. Institutions allow this monolithic culture to politely exclude these students from the mainstream of campus culture. The second stage involves coexisting but separate minority subcultures within the dominant campus culture. During this stage, a college allows groups to conduct a Black History Month or Cinco de Mayo celebration, but they make no other attempts to integrate students' cultures or ideas, especially in the classroom. During the third stage, however, separate subcultures merge with the dominant campus culture to form an integrated campus community that respects the uniqueness of each subcultural group.

Most college campuses continue to struggle with moving their institutions into the third stage, as Cross suggests, so that their retention rates for students of color can improve. Institutions are looking for approaches, techniques, and classroom enhancements that integrate students of color into the campus community. Positive cultural experiences are desirable because they reduce fear and distrust among campus racial and cultural groups, and produce a campus cultural synergy that facilitates social interactions outside of the classroom. Despite these presumed advantages, scholars are still uncertain as to the real value of a multicultural campus environment.

Multicultural strategies and programs represent increased access to educational, economical, social, and political opportunities in a democratic society. Multiculturalism includes a diversified body of knowledge that represents cultural values and traditions. It also involves presenting the historical, cultural, political, sociological, economical, and educational contributions that diverse groups have had on the development and growth of our country and world (Banks, 1989).

2

INSTITUTIONAL CHARACTERISTICS AND PROFILES

Multicultural colleges aim to provide their students with an environment in which the faculty, administrators, and students come together to share knowledge and to provide contexts for further application of ideas in order to help the world become a better place. Dynamic multicultural colleges embody in their missions and cultures many of the characteristics that Birnbaum (1988) identifies in his collegial model: "[a]n emphasis on consensus, shared, power, common commitments and aspirations, and leadership that emphasizes consultation and collective responsibilities . . ." (p. 86).

The seven colleges included in this study exhibit many of the characteristics detailed in Birnbaum's (1988) collegiate model:

. . . not an institution in which hierarchy is considered to be very important, and much of the interaction among members of the collegium is informal in nature. The college is egalitarian and democratic, and members of the administration and faculty consider each other as equals, all of whom have the right and opportunity for discussion and influence as issues come up. Like some other collegial bodies, the faculty and administration of . . . are concerned about the views of nonmembers such as staff and students, but the right of these others to participation is severely circumscribed and often only token in nature. (p. 88)

. . . as does any collegial group, has an administration to provide support services and to represent the college's interests to its various publics, but the administration is understood to be subordinate to the collegium and carries out the collegium's will. Administrators are often members of the faculty who agree to serve for a limited time and then return to their classroom responsibilities. Administrators therefore tend to be "amateurs," rather than professionals. (p. 88)

Collegiality, seen as a community of individuals with shared interests, can probably be maintained only where regular face-to-face contact provides the necessary coordinating mechanisms and where programs and traditions are integrated enough to permit the development of a coherent culture. (p. 93)

The social forces that develop common attitudes, activities, and norms are not available to a large institution in the same way as they are to a small one. But even if many colleges and universities are not truly communities governed through collegial structures, the concept of the collegial model as an ideal type may have significant consequences for the way in which these institutions are controlled. (pp. 93–94)

Collegium members interact and influence each other through a network of continuous personal exchanges based on social attraction, value consensus, and reciprocity. (p. 94)

Because all the institutions in the study may be classified as small, unique, liberal arts colleges or universities, a framework to classify these institutions seems warranted. Each college's mission and philosophy are cited in this chapter. Although the missions and philosophies of these seven colleges have distinct differences, they have striking similarities with regard to their commitment to (1) promoting high expectations of their students, (2) advancing global educational experiences, (3) developing responsible and respectful individuals who give back to their community and world, (4) opening dialog in order to understand multiple perspectives, and (5) supporting multiple cultures and differences within and outside of the classroom.

Though Birnbaum's (1988) notion of the collegiate model is introduced, it is faulty to assume that every college will fit neatly into this paradigm. In fact, the most unique quality about the institutions in the study is that they each strive to generate new and creative ways to approach challenges, ways that by all intents and purposes could be recognized as dynamic.

What follows is a snapshot of the institutions and their profiles so that the reader can better understand the context in which the students' voices are shaped. Each college is presented in alphabetical order. The data used for institutional profiles were obtained from various institutional offices, websites, popular publications, and other resources. For the purpose of this book, however, pseudonyms are used to protect the students' and institutions' identities. Hence, the profiles of the institutions have been greatly altered so that they might remain anonymous. Therefore, if the name of an actual college does exist that matches the pseudonyms selected, it is by coincidence. Table 2.1 serves as a reference point so that readers can easily compare the institutions and their characteristics.

Table 2.1

Characteristics of Colleges by Ranges for Comparison

Description	Faculty	SAT/ACT	Expenses	FAF	Enrollment	Diversity (%)	Setting
Balsam	160–175	1250–1460	$21,000–$25,000	$ 3080–$25,500	1700–1900	Black (3) American Indian (1) Asian (7.9) Unknown (4.7) White (82.8)	Small town in rural area; 60 miles to major city
Cedar	190–200	1250–1410	$20,500–$25,000	NSAG*	2730–3000	Black (4) American Indian (1) Asian (4) Hispanic (3) White (88)	Small town; less than 30 miles to major city
Elm	75–95	1200–1250/ 24–28	$18,000–$23,000	NSAG*	1000–1500	Black (4.9) American Indian (1) Asian (2.7) Hispanic (1.2) White (91)	Small to midsize town; less than 60 miles to major city
Hickory	85–100	1080–1340	$18,500–$23,500	$2678–$16,500	1150–1300	Black (5.4) American Indian (1)	Small town; more than 180 miles

						Asian (4.7) Hispanic (3.7) White (80) Unknown (4.7)	to major city
Pine	115–125	1100–1250	$20,000–$25,000	NSAG*	1600–1800	Black (6) American Indian (1) Asian (17) Hispanic (20) White (56)	Suburban area between two small cities
Redwood	60–75	1150–1230/ 23–28	$21,700–$28,000	$8225–$18,560	860–950	Black (6.6) American Indian (1) Asian (10.8) Hispanic (13.8) White (56)	Suburban area; less than 25 miles to major city
Sycamore	330–350	1100–1300	$21,900–$27,000	NSAG*	3200–3350	Black (7.3) American Indian (0) Asian (9.2) Hispanic (5.5) White (77.2)	Small town; more than than 120 miles to major city

*No specific amount given; however, tries to meet all needs of students who qualify based on need and merit.

Note: Faculty is full-time status around the average number reported. SAT/ACT is in range format around the mean. FAF range is based on institutional, federal, and state funding from smallest amount awarded to largest amount awarded. Diversity of student body is based on reported round numbers, therefore, the total may not add up to 100 percent.

Balsam College

Balsam College, located in a small town, is an independent, four-year, coeducational liberal arts institution awarding bachelor degrees in more than thirty different majors. Students come from fifty-three states and territories in addition to twenty different countries. The student population is split evenly between males (50 percent) and females (50 percent). Eighty-three percent of the students live on campus; on-campus residency is required for the first year and at least one additional year. Fifty-nine percent of the students have need-based financial aid, approximately 17 percent of the students are minorities, 95 percent of the 1994 full-time freshmen class returned for a second year, and 90 percent of the student population graduates within six years.

According to its mission, Balsam College challenges its students by providing a liberal education of the highest quality, preparing them to lead rewarding, creative, and useful lives. Balsam's academic structure is built upon a set of basic skills that includes perceptive reading, clear written and verbal communication, and analytical thinking.

The Balsam curriculum focuses on classic fields of study, training students to challenge themselves against the major time-tested structures of intellectual inquiry. Added to the curriculum are interdisciplinary courses that aid students in the application of skills to questions requiring broad-based approaches—approaches utilizing many disciplines. The college also requires students to distribute their courses among four divisions of knowledge, take at least one course concerning another culture, and demonstrate proficiency in English composition and in a second language. Balsam also encourages students to study abroad and to participate actively in the creative and performing arts and athletics.

The culture at Balsam is one that values family, loyalty, learning, and knowledge, as well as the individual. Every student is guaranteed housing, with 83 percent of the student population living on campus, a sign that students are near their living quarters. There is a sense of family and loyalty at Balsam, expressed by the fact that faculty members advise students. The school is also homogeneous in its thinking and population, with a bent toward conservatism. It is an institution where teaching comes first, and the liberal arts core curriculum is highly valued. Balsam is a place where most people will know or at least be familiar with almost everyone else on campus, and where diversity in thought and, more recently, in the student population, is prized.

Cedar University

Cedar University's mission is to provide a dynamic educational experience to a select group of diverse, talented, intellectually sophisticated students who are capable of challenging themselves, their peers, and their teachers in a setting that brings together living and learning. Cedar is a highly selective, independent, coeducational liberal arts college that enrolls approximately 2,750 undergraduate students seeking bachelor of arts degrees. A small graduate program offers the master of arts and the master of arts in teaching degrees.

Cedar's curriculum is centered on four academic divisions—humanities, natural sciences and mathematics, social sciences, and university studies. Cedar encourages a well-rounded variety of academic experiences by offering forty-eight undergraduate concentrations (majors). Competency for all students must be demonstrated in a foreign or classical language, and in English composition. A student of Cedar declares a major during the second year and an optional minor usually during the third year of enrollment. The Cedar educational experiences emphasize an international perspective for all students. The university offers seven modern and two classical languages as well as several off-campus study programs, most of which are operated overseas. Cedar's academic programs prepare students for many careers, including professions that require graduate school training.

Cedar is a residential university located in a small town with a population of approximately 2,500 residents. Cedar's faculty, administrators, students, and the residents of the town share the responsibility for encouraging all members of the university community to actively engage in all aspects of the learning process and support Cedar's mission statement.

Residential life at Cedar is also an enriching experience for students, as it has eight traditional residence halls, fraternity and sorority chapter homes, apartment communities, and a host of unique living communities. The living communities vary according to ethnicity, academic programs, and political and social issues, including homes where each semester the students choose their own theme. Some houses have strong ties to specific academic programs, but each house has one or more faculty fellows. As a group, residents of every house independently plan and present a series of social, cultural, and educational events designed to promote the sense of community within the house and across the university.

Elm College

Elm College is a private liberal arts institution located in a small town. Its mission is to produce brilliant intellectuals and citizens who are committed to their society. Elm seems content to reveal itself through its religious order heritage and more modern curriculum and program offerings. The belief that each student has individual worth that is neither greater nor less than that of any other student is a concept not foreign to most colleges and universities. It is, in fact, a principle rooted in American democracy. What separates Elm from most other colleges and universities, however, is the belief that every community member at Elm is viewed as an equal.

Elm College provides many opportunities for cross-cultural education and exchanges between students. The Office of Multicultural Affairs is the primary support office, but many other offices also support this ideal. The Cultural Center serves as a residence for students and also sponsors educational and cultural programming. The Office of Residential Life provides other residence halls and houses which promote cultural exchanges. Unique living communities are encouraged with regard to ethnicity, interests, and academics. Classes, films, traditional meals, and speakers or programs also are held during the year in various living and learning communities.

Hickory College

Hickory College is a small, four-year liberal arts college located in a town of 35,000 people. Students arrive on campus from over forty states and more than thirty countries, providing the campus with a variety of cultural backgrounds. Academically speaking, Hickory students are predominantly from the top quartile of their high school graduating classes, making the admission process fairly selective. Several themes flow through the mission statement of Hickory College, particularly that of diversity. The initial paragraph points to the goal of individuals of diverse backgrounds to challenge each other to explore, understand, and improve oneself, one's society, and the world.

The mission statement also describes a commitment to active liberal arts education, with an emphasis on student engagement in the educational process. This ideal is reflected in the philosophy of encouraging students to pursue fundamental questions to reach their own reflective but independent judgments. This approach is also augmented by a policy of challenging students with high expectations within a supportive framework.

Pine College

Pine College is located midway between two small cities. Both cities include popular retail stores, restaurants, and movie theaters less than a ten-minute drive from campus. The enrollment demographics of Pine College are representative of the community in which it is located; however, the percentage of minority students at Pine College is not similar to the national average of college enrollments. The national average is 7.9 percent Latino, 5.8 percent Asian American, 10.7 percent African American, 1.0 percent Native American, and 74.7 percent White. Although the Native American population of students at Pine mirrors national averages, the institution has a higher percentage of Latino and Asian American students. The institution has a lower percentage of African American students and a significantly lower percentage of White students.

Pine College's mission focuses on interdisciplinarism and multiculturalism. The school claims that this program seeks to foster both the fulfillment of individual aspirations and the deeply rooted commitments to the public good. Pine fosters this fulfillment by providing a gifted and diverse group of students with a total educational experience of the highest quality.

The large minority population on campus promotes a multicultural environment. Pine remains aware of the needs and issues of the different ethnicities by encouraging the celebration of diversity. One example is by setting aside the days, weeks, and months to educate students about the different cultures represented on campus. The academic culture of the institution is highly challenging. Students spend most of their time studying, which affects their social life on campus. Many identified an internal rather than an external competitiveness as the source of their drive to succeed.

Redwood College

Redwood College is situated in a city with a population of 35,000. Redwood has a reputation for effectively combining research and teaching. The institution is a coeducational, liberal arts institution offering a bachelor of arts degree with an emphasis in the social and behavioral sciences. As for student geographic background, 60 percent of the students are from within the state, 4.6 percent are international students, and the remaining 35 percent are from outside the state.

Students are required to live on campus through their junior year; currently 68 percent of the students live on campus. Special campus buildings include the Black and Chicano study centers, women's center, theater arts center, and coffeehouse. Redwood typifies a small, private, liberal arts school that is thriving in a midsize community. What differentiates Redwood from peer institutions is its educational philosophy, educational objectives, and contemporary approach to achieving these objectives. Redwood's educational philosophy is singular and corresponds with its heritage. Faculty members strive to enhance individual growth and at the same time build community. Redwood faculty pioneered the increasingly popular approach of looking at issues from the perspectives of multiple cultures and from the points of view of several disciplines, using this diverse knowledge to make the world a better place. The curriculum and campus life encourage the union of intellect with action, by providing opportunities to test theory, practice techniques, and explore career options through campus governance, internships, and study-abroad programs.

Sycamore University

Sycamore is considered to be one of the top liberal arts universities. It is located in the northeastern United States, about 120 miles from two major metropolitan cities. The population of the town where Sycamore is located is approximately 43,000, and the minority populace comprises about 20 percent of this constituency. Sycamore's curriculum consists of 960 courses, from forty-two departments, and forty-seven major fields of study. The curriculum includes courses in ethnic backgrounds such as African American studies. Sycamore offers only one undergraduate degree, the bachelor of arts. It also offers a master's and a doctoral degree; the master of arts is granted in seven fields of study and the doctoral of philosophy is granted in six fields of study. Sycamore's mission is to educate its students in a variety of ways and to prepare them for the future. For example, the institution offers them intellectual independence and the ability to link distinct fields of learning through critical thinking.

The university provides financial assistance to those students in need. Most of the students admitted to Sycamore receive financial aid. In addition, it provides student loans, fellowships, scholarships, and work study for minority students and others who are unable to receive financial aid or need more financial assistance. Any student who is admitted to Sycamore can expect to receive financial aid based on need for a minimum of four years.

In summary, one should be cautious regarding the transferability of programs, services, and curricula from one context to another in conjunction with the institutions and students cited in this study. The degree to which the stories and institutional uniqueness can be applied to contexts beyond those in which they develop depends on the similarity between the two contexts. Hence, the rationale for detailed descriptions of these institutions becomes important for transferability (Lincoln and Guba, 1985).

3

RESEARCH METHODS
AND PROCEDURES
FOR INQUIRY

The overall significance of any study is never realized fully until one understands the research methods and procedures used in the research investigation. This fact is particularly important when conducting qualitative research where the research methods and processes for data gathering and data coding are often unique to the participant group or phenomenon being studied. The purpose of this chapter is to outline and describe the qualitative methods and procedures utilized in this study of multicultural students. Included within this discussion is a description of the focus group and interview procedures. The first step to understanding and assigning meaning to the collegiate experiences of the multicultural students in this study is to characterize that process known as qualitative research.

Characteristics of Qualitative Research

Qualitative research implies a scientific inquiry method that places an emphasis on processes and meanings (Denzin and Lincoln, 1994). Such research does not examine, or measure, in terms of quantity, amount, intensity, or frequency. Rather, "qualitative researchers stress the socially constructed nature of reality, the intimate relationship between the researcher and what is studied, and the situational constraints that shape inquiry" (p. 8).

Creswell (1998) extended this definition by noting that qualitative research is a method of inquiry that explores a social or human problem. For the present study, the concern is, How do college campuses create multicultural learning environments? Once created, how do these campuses then support and promote the personal development of their multicultural students? The qualitative researcher seeks to build a holistic picture of informants, or participants, in a natural setting.

Qualitative researchers seek answers to questions that emphasize how social experience is created and given meaning (Denzin and Lincoln, 1994). In our present study, we sought to discover how multicultural students' social experiences are created and how the students assign meaning to their social and academic experiences. Following that discovery, the present study identified those campus climate characteristics that support or promote multiculturalism.

Capturing the Voice of the Students

Qualitative research assigns value to the "voice" of the participants—in this case, the multicultural students on each of the seven selected college campuses. Qualitative research models seek to uncover patterns of relationships among the voices of participants within the community. Researchers seek a holistic understanding of how participants within the phenomenon construct meaning and use this newly created framework in a practical manner. Our study uncovered patterns of relationship among the multicultural students on each respective campus and noted ways they assigned meaning to their collegiate experiences. Qualitative research models seek to understand the relational patterns of students' involvement within the phenomenon under study, that is, the college environment. We sought to discover how multicultural students have experiences within their college campuses and to learn what meaning is constructed from that involvement.

Examining Institutional Climate

Qualitative methods are useful for examining institutional factors and capturing student interactional characteristics. Such institutional factors as culture or climate, norms, beliefs, and mission can be codified using qualitative methods (Whitt and Kuh, 1991). They are highly appropriate for studying factors within colleges (Lincoln and Guba, 1985; Patton, 1990), especially those within student affairs (Kuh and Andreas, 1991), because it improves administrators' understanding of individual and groups of students. Unlike quantitative research, which yields numbers that categorize student behaviors, qualitative research yields words as data that capture students' experiences (Kuh and Andreas, 1991). Grounded in the daily experiences of college students, qualitative research is particularly powerful because it represents an active interface between the investigator(s) and the participants (students).

Qualitative research is an active process whereby researchers interact with their research participants for the purpose of discovering aspects of their lives and experiences. Through the various qualitative methods and processes of inquiry, researchers learn how individuals construct and assign meaning within the context of the phenomenon under study. For the current investigation, the authors sought to understand how multicultural students experienced their colleges; and, as a result of that interaction, how they later assigned meaning to their college experience. Throughout the remainder of this chapter, we inform the reader about the research procedures and methods used to gather rich information and data about multicultural students' experiences on small, predominantly White, American college campuses. The following pages detail the steps taken in this investigation.

Operating Assumptions

This research blends two theoretical traditions to help understand multicultural students who are attending American colleges: student development theory and multicultural approaches. This plan is no accident. These two philosophical approaches offer the researcher a strong conceptual framework upon which to assign meaning and practical application to this important work regarding multicultural students. The researchers operated throughout this study within the framework of student development theory and multiculturalism. From this blended theoretical framework comes six philosophical assumptions that guided this research inquiry from research design to data collection to interpretation and the assignment of meaning.

1. Multicultural students proceed through a definable set of developmental phases as they progress throughout the college years.

2. Multicultural students learn and grow best when they are involved in their campus communities, and that involvement is valued by the institution.

3. Multicultural students learn and develop in a variety of ways within and outside the formal classroom setting.

4. Multicultural students interact with their campus environments in ways that encourage their personal development and promote their learning.

5. Campus climate has a direct impact on multicultural students' experiences in college and how they thrive in their learning communities.

6. Multicultural students change colleges in significant and positive ways that enhance the entire campus community.

These philosophical assumptions shaped the context of this study and, for this reason, it is necessary to identify conceptual and/or operational biases now. These biases shaped the manner with which we viewed multicultural students, because we believe multicultural students *change* colleges. These assumptions shaped our inquiry in four ways.

1. We chose not to compare multicultural students with Euro-American students because such comparisons, historically, have left multicultural students being the least valued.

2. We valued the voice of students "as is." As a result, the researchers did not try to change, alter, or otherwise influence students' perceptions of their campus environments.

3. We chose not to contextualize students' comments using institutional terms such as *retention*. Instead, we used descriptions and phrases that arose from within the students' learning environments.

4. We were careful not to homogenize, or tone down, students' statements. By doing so, we would have lessened the value and potency of their comments. Just suppose, for example, that a student remarked during an interview that the campus "sucked." We did not categorize it as simply a "bad" experience. If we had changed the phrase (to sound more politically correct, we would have changed the meaning in its social context), and that would lessen its meaning for the student.

We make no excuses for these assumptions. They are presented here within the context of our research methodology, because it is ethically responsible to do so as a qualitative researcher. The responsible researcher identifies or articulates preconceptions, biases, or assumptions early on to all stakeholders in the research inquiry. Therefore, we chose to maintain the integrity of students' voices and exercised great care in our data analysis and coding.

Involvement is a two-way dialogue between the multicultural students and all campus participants, including students, faculty, staff, and community. This research study was designed to help student affairs professionals understand the nature of this transaction so as to maximize the learning experience for their students. With these operating assumptions as a context, the next step is to outline the inquiry process used and to describe the procedures and methods employed for gathering data.

Research Design

Four basic questions guided this study: (1) How do multicultural students experience their colleges? (2) How do they characterize such experiences? (3) How does campus climate shape students' learning, especially outside of the classroom? (4) How does racial identity influence students and the way in which they experience their college campuses?

The present study combined phenomenological and ethnographic methods to investigate these four core research questions regarding multicultural students' college experiences. The blending of these qualitative methodologies allowed the research team to fully capture the students' voices accurately.

"Phenomenology describes the meaning of multicultural students' lived experiences within their particular college setting" (Creswell, 1998, p. 51). It captures and explores the structure of consciousness of human experiences (Polkinghorne, 1989, cited in Creswell, 1998). From this framework, the research team created questions that ask students to explore the meaning of their college experiences, looking for their underlying meaning. Borrowing from psychological phenomenology, which seeks to discover the meaning of individual experiences rather than group experiences, it employs a series of steps in the data analysis to ascertain the realm of the students' college experiences (Creswell, 1998).

Ethnography seeks to describe and interpret the experiences of a cultural group or social system. In this instance, we wanted to learn about multicultural students, as a social or cultural group in our chosen colleges (Creswell, 1998). Ethnography typically requires that the researcher interact with students for a prolonged period of time as part of the investigation. Although we did not have the opportunity to study each campus extensively, we searched for a holistic understanding of multicultural students as a social group on campus. We modified the traditional ethnographic analysis by using multiple sites to examine multicultural students as a social group. In this regard, the research team modified and redesigned traditional ethnographic investigation methods to fit the parameters of this study. The advantage of borrowing from ethnography lies in the discovery of a holistic portrait of multicultural students as they live daily on small college campuses across America.

The blending of these two powerful qualitative research traditions provided a storehouse of potent interview and data analysis techniques and approaches from which came rich details about multicultural students' daily lives. Additionally, we sought to reveal a holistic portrait of multicultural students and gained a comprehensive and complete picture of them as they experience predominantly White, small college campuses. In doing so, we learned about the group's sociopolitical history, their cultural worldviews, career aspirations, perceptions of and value for their families, social support networks, and personal legacy to these colleges.

Introduction to Research Design

The current study was conducted in two distinct phases. The first phase involved presenting a model for institutional selection of campus sites and describing procedures and methods of gaining entry onto each campus. The second phase involved gathering data from dozens of multicultural students across all college campuses selected. The second phase included focus groups and individual student interviews, survey data, and other campus-relevant artifacts and observational notes from the researchers involved.

The full procedures describing each phase of this project are outlined throughout the remainder of this chapter.

Colleges move through various stages in their efforts to develop themselves as a multicultural campus. As institutions become aware of multicultural students' needs, they take steps to remove such barriers for them. Once committed to multiculturalism, colleges become intentional and purposeful in their efforts toward the creation of a multicultural learning environment.

Selecting Colleges

We utilized three instruments for selecting the colleges that were included within this study. These measures were developed by researchers at the Higher Educational Research Institute at the University of California, Los Angeles, and are related to issues of diversity or multiculturalism. The three research instruments are institutional diversity emphasis (IDE), faculty diversity emphasis (FDE), and student diversity experiences (SDEs). The first two measures are based upon the responses of the faculty at 289 institutions to an extensive questionnaire administered during the 1992–1993 academic year. The third selection measure was developed using five items from the 1991 follow-up questionnaire of 1987 freshman. Table 3.1 provides survey items for each measure. Note that the FDE is based on the faculty's own scholarly and pedagogic practices, whereas IDE reflects faculty's perceptions of the overall institutional climate. The latter measure reflects not only faculty values and behaviors, but also the policies of the administration and the governance.

On the basis of their responses to two institutional surveys, twelve colleges were chosen initially for inclusion in this study. Five colleges were excluded from this study for a variety of reasons pertaining to administrative changes or budgetary consideration. The data from one school were incomplete and thus not included in our final study. Ultimately, seven colleges were selected for participation, but for reasons of confidentiality, they are described throughout the book using pseudonyms. These

Table 3.1

Measures to Select Participating Institutions

Institutional Diversity Emphasis	Faculty Diversity Emphasis	Student Diversity Experiences
• To increase the number of minority faculty • To increase the number of minority students • To create a diverse multicultural environment • To increase the number of women faculty • To develop an appreciation for multiculturalism	• To enhance instructional techniques that incorporate reading on racial and ethnic issues • To enhance instructional techniques that incorporate reading on women and gender • To perform research or writing that focuses on racial and ethnic minorities • To perform research or writing that focuses on women and gender	• Took ethnic studies courses • Took women's studies courses • Attended racial and cultural awareness workshops • Discussed racial and ethnic issues • Socialized with someone from another racial or ethnic group

schools are best characterized as small, private, liberal arts colleges located throughout the continental United States. Each of these schools is known by its strong academic reputation, but not well known for diversity of enrollment or experience.

Gaining Entry onto College Campuses

College Presidents Entry onto each institution's campus began with the multicultural research team first contacting the college president or chief academic officer by way of a formal letter of invitation (Appendix A). The purpose of this letter was twofold. First, this letter introduced the multicultural research team project to the college president and described the proposed research activities scheduled to occur. Second, the letter extended an official invitation for the college to become involved in this research study. A short research project description and a proposed timetablefor data collection on the campus was provided. A follow-up phone contact from a research team member helped to clarify any questions or concerns of the college president. Once the college president agreed to allow the institution to become involved, the research team started the active process of entering the campus.

Campus Contact Personnel   The president usually designated a student affairs staff professional, (i.e., assistant to the president or the dean of students) to serve as the contact liaison for this research endeavor. The campus designee assisted the team members in prearrival preparation, facilitated contact with students, and set interview appointments. In short, this campus designee became the project's contact person for all matters on campus.

Campus Research Review Procedures   The research project was approved earlier by each of the multicultural research team's home institutions. Despite this fact, we believed it important to seek research approval from each participating institution's research review board. Because the participating institutions were small, private, liberal arts colleges, most did not require further application to other research review committees. Our participating colleges accepted the consent forms previously developed and approved by the team's home institutions, which meant the team did not seek any additional research approval. The informed consent procedures for students are described in this chapter (see Appendix B for a sample consent form). Each participating college president received a statement of general assurance, which outlined the ways in which the institutional research would be used by the team, and a research booklet, which described the procedures to be employed and contained the research consent form.

Role of Multicultural Research Team Project Staff

The research team project staff handled all administrative matters and organizational details related to institutional visitation. This staff ensured that all travel and interview arrangements were completed upon arrival of the research team. The project team staff coordinated the scheduling of campus visits and the assignment of research team members to schools, which was completed prior to the first college interview. Once on the campus, the researcher was responsible for collecting the institutional and student surveys, demographic information, and other research project materials such as collateral materials and artifacts. The researcher made certain that all tapes and other materials were transported in a secure manner back to the project team staff personnel designated to do tape transcription.

Selection of Students

Selecting multicultural students depended upon the collaboration and cooperation of the participating institutions. The designated campus professional assumed the leadership to identify students for participation in this study. The campus professionals selected students in several ways: (1) by personal contact and invitation, (2) by notice sent via e-mail or list serve, (3) by naming recognized student leaders, (4) through word of mouth from students themselves, and (5) by recommendation from faculty, staff, or other students.

During the recruitment process, the campus professional informed prospective student participants about the exact nature of the study, including the parameters and time commitment involved. Students were given an opportunity to ask general questions about the study and anonymity safeguards. Approximately 150 students were selected as participants in this study, across all seven college campuses. Most of the students were of traditional age and lived on campus, and classification included freshmen to seniors.

Data Gathering

Data gathering involves a variety of activities to collect research data concerning multicultural students' experiences of each respective campus. Consistent with phenomenology and ethnography models, several data gathering activities were employed for this study. Although the primary method of gathering information was through individual and/or small-group interviews, other research methods used were as follows:

- Collecting printed materials concerning student activities, programs, and services
- Observing interactions in real-life settings such as classrooms or residence halls
- Noting verbal comments from staff, faculty, and students
- Observing nonverbal communication styles
- Noting patterns of electronic communication and students' relationships to technology
- Recording notes taken by research investigators
- Collecting survey data

These multimethod data gathering techniques were intended to encompass totally the student's lived experiences during college. The multimethod approach also allowed the researchers to capture students' voices accurately. In the pages that follow, the specific details and processes of data gathering are described, beginning with a discussion of the instrumentation used throughout the study.

Instrumentation

One survey, the Racial Identity Scale, was used along with a demographic sheet. Each is described here briefly. These instruments were usually completed prior to the start of the focus group meeting.

1. *Racial Identity Scale (revised).* Developed by Thomas Parham and Janet Helms (1981, 1985), this scale was designed to measure racial identity attitudes reflective of the states of racial identity development proposed by Cross (1978). This test assesses an individual's placement among a variety of worldviews, each stage having distinctive racial identity attitudes consisting of cognitive and affective complements (Parham and Helms, 1985). This scale has been adapted for use with other racial and cultural groups. In general, obtained reliability scores were moderate and compared favorably with those obtained on nonculture-specific personality measures (Anastasi, 1985). Obtained reliabilities for the short form are as follows for each subscale: pre-encounter = .69; encounter = .50; immersion/emmersion = .67. This form was modified for use in this study.

2. *Demographic information.* Participants completed a demographic information sheet (Appendix C) after the Racial Identity Scale. This form asks for basic information about students' background such as year in school, family of origin, college major, and self-identified cultural or racial group membership.

Interviews

During this study, small-group interviews served as the primary method of gathering information. In some cases, individual student interviews occurred when large groups did not materialize. The student focus groups were held in campus locations deemed appropriate by the campus professional. Locations such as conference or meeting rooms in the student union, dean of students' office, or residential life learning centers were used. These meeting rooms were selected because they offered privacy for participants. Once student participants arrived at the location designed for the interview, they were given a research packet of materials and asked to complete them prior to the start of the interview. Four items were included in the research packet: a research consent form, a demographic information sheet, the Racial Identity Scale, and mailing addresses and general information regarding the principal investigators.

Once seated in the interview room, student participants were asked to read and sign the consent form. Any general questions regarding the study were answered at this time before students completed any forms or were interviewed. The exact interview procedures and interview question protocol are detailed in Appendices D and E. Students were asked to read and sign the research consent form. All consent forms were collected from participants and sealed in an envelope. Signing of the consent form was done prior to the interview or completion of any demographic information. Next, participants were instructed to complete the Racial Identity Scale and the demographic information sheet. Together these forms took approximately twenty minutes to complete. Once completed, participants returned the forms to the researcher who placed them in separate envelopes.

The researcher then briefly explained the nature of the study and clarified questions. The researcher stressed the respondents' anonymity. All interviews were recorded on tape using two cassette tape recorders with external omnidirectional microphones. Once the consent and survey data were returned to the researcher, the tape recorders were turned on and the interview commenced.

The researcher proceeded to asked questions of participants using a semistructured interview format as described in Appendix F. The questions used in the open-ended interview survey were presented in the same order to each interview group across all college settings. Following the open-ended interview questions, an informal conversational interview was used to gather additional data from the participants. These interview questions were used to prompt the participants in hopes of uncovering information not discovered during the semistructured interview phase.

According to Patton (1990), it is possible to adopt a standardized open-ended interview format in the early part of an interview and then leave the interviewer free to pursue any subjects of interest during the latter parts of the interview. The informal conversational interview was unstructured and provided us with maximum flexibility to permit the data to naturally emerge through casual discourse. The informal conversational interview questions were not uniform across respondents.

Researchers also took notes during each interview to record the nonverbal and situational cues that often are not recorded on tape. Taking notes forces one to listen and hear the main point, and provides backup in case of technological problems. When taking notes, the researcher is able to write possible questions to use later in the interview (Rubin and Rubin, 1995).

Once the interviews ended, the researcher provided student participants with a short debriefing about the full nature of the study. Students were reminded again that any follow-up questions could be directed to the research interviewer or any research team project member. Student participants were told that, upon completion of the study, each would receive a written summary of the study's findings and outcomes.

While visiting each college campus, the researcher used this time to gather other written data and artifacts, such as college admissions materials, departmental descriptions of courses, and information about campus services including multicultural and international student support services.

Managing and Recording Data

The researchers (or designated agents) transcribed all of the interview data. Once a researcher completed an interview, the tapes and raw data were sent to the research team office for storage until ready for transcription.

The transcribed tape recorded information was stored on computer disks, rather than on a computer hard drive. All transcription cassettes, and other written material were stored in a locked file cabinet, inaccessible to anyone except the designated clerical or graduate assistant and the researcher. The tapes were transcribed on a standalone computer; and were not filed on a network server because no security encryption was available at the time of this research. Transcribers used pseudonyms or numbers rather than names to identify research participants, to protect anonymity.

Data Analysis Strategies

Data analysis involves the detailed, timely process of discovering themes from and assigning meaning to the interview data from multicultural students on all seven college campuses. As Miles and Huberman (1994, cited in Creswell, 1998, p. 142) observed, data analysis is not "off-the-shelf." It is custom built, revised, and "choreographed." Data analysis begins with the organization of the interview materials. At the earliest phase of the project, researchers convert their files to appropriate text units (e.g., a word, phrase, sentence, or long story) for analysis. Data generated from the twenty-five campus interviews were voluminous and took months to code and analyze. The vast array of interview data helped ensure that our collection of information truly saturated the phenomenon of students' lived experiences at college.

The first step was to identify general themes or categories from the interview data. Strauss and Corbin (1990) define a data category as a unit of information comprised of events, happenings, and occurrences. In the present study, we searched for categories of information that represented the following theme areas.

- Perceptions of the campus and its mission
- Campus culture
- Impressions about the student body in general
- Impressions about one's own peer group
- Feelings about self (self-esteem)
- Perceptions about self as a student of color (including racial identification)

- Learning environment within classroom
- Interactions between and among students (on campus)
- Interactions among group members (small-group interview)
- Relationship between interviewer and group members
- Future view of self
- Relationship with faculty and staff within/outside classroom

Later, the interview data were divided into statements that represented the above-mentioned areas. This process of horizontalization occurs when original protocols are divided into general categories. Here, twelve categories were transformed later into clusters of meanings, expressed in psychological and phenomenological principles or concepts (Creswell, 1998). In general, these new clusters of information used language that was most consistent with students' vernacular and worldviews. The categories are as follows:

- What you see is what you get. (reality of campus culture)
- Ask anyone—they'll tell you. (perceptions of campus and its mission)
- So, where's the professor? (lack of diversity in professors)
- If I can make it there, I can make it anywhere. (coping statements and self-beliefs)
- R-e-s-p-e-c-t: Find out what it means to me. (campus perceptions of students)
- If this world were mine . . . (involvement, future views of self)

Finally, we tied together these transformed definitions to create a (new) textural description of multicultural students' perceptions of their colleges and redesigned a structural description of how these students actually experienced college. Since the researchers are themselves multicultural faculty and staff professionals residing within college environments similar to those of our student participants, we incorporated our personal meaning into our data analysis. In this regard, we became participant-observers during these interviews. We ourselves had similar cultural learning experiences to our students under study, only a generation ago. Our worldviews and lived college experiences contributed to the way in which we assign meaning and interpreted the study's findings by analyzing the role of race, culture, and language barriers in the lives of these college students.

When taken together, the end product of this data analysis allowed the research team to reveal a single unifying theme underlying these interviews: Multicultural students wish to thrive, grow, and develop themselves while at college. They are keenly aware that their colleges have restricting relational patterns and structural barriers that exist to limit their self-perceptions of and actual movement toward student developmental goals.

INTRODUCTION
TO CHAPTERS 4 THROUGH 6

The purpose of this study was to address the following questions: (1) How do minority undergraduates experience learning
outside the classroom? How do they characterize such experiences? (2) How does racial identity influence minority students'
learning experiences outside the classroom? (3) How does campus climate influence minorities' out-of-classroom learning? To
uncover these responses, we asked some additional questions,
such as: What campus-based initiatives were in place to assist
the multicultural student in his/her transition to the collegiate
environment? What services did the university provide to
address the unique social and cultural needs of the multicultural
student? Did the university acknowledge and promote multiculturalism and diversity among its student population through
special programming initiatives?

In light of the fact that these are students' voices, one must remember that the institutions chosen for this study are already outstanding in their approach to multicultural awareness and practices, identified by criteria cited earlier in the book. Regardless of how well most institutions are performing with their services for students of color, there continues to be room for improvement. The students' perceptions and testimonies are not criticisms of the institutions, but depictions of individual experiences and sense-making of these experiences. Students' backgrounds and prior exposure to institutions of higher education equally influence the way they experience the world and multiple institutional agents within the campus environment. It should be noted that "for any, individual student, the specific college he or she attends can, indeed, be very important" (Kuh, 1992, p. 352). In fact, Watson and Kuh (1996) found that even though Black students might be more involved in campus activities than White students, they reap less from their academic experiences at some private predominantly White institutions. The difference of race in our institutions of higher education partially indicates that the type of college does make a difference for many students.

In 1978, the Southern Regional Education Board (SREB) conducted a study on students attending predominantly "other race" institutions. The conclusion from the study was that students who were in the minority were convinced that the "trade off" is worthwhile and that the educational gains were much greater than the "extra effort, struggle, or consideration necessary to achieve their educational goals in an 'other race' institution" (Abraham and Jacobs, 1990, p. 24). To the contrary, the SREB duplicated the study in 1990 and found that there were more negative attitudes from minority students than in the previous study. Students from both predominantly White and historically Black institutions are less willing to make the "trade off" than their cohorts from the 1970s (Abraham and Jacobs, 1990). In simple terms, these findings indicate that Black and White students are not willing to put up with the hassle of suffering psychologically in order to attend an institution that neither welcomes nor appreciates their culture and heritage.

Interviews with students of color continue to show them to be plagued with feelings of isolation, inadequacies, distrust, and adjustment problems to college. Most of them believe that, due to their racial and ethnic characteristics, they have an additional challenge while attending predominantly White, private institutions.

This study sheds light on issues relative to how we might begin to view both the educational experiences and outcomes of minority students. In Chapters 4 through 7, patterns may be discovered that encapsulate these students' experiences. This is a preferred approach, rather than developing conclusive statements about all minority students and all institutions. Hence, "as each person provides a context for other stories, they together discover, recognize, or create patterns to make sense of their collective experiences" (Magolda, 1993, p. 17).

Magolda (1992) reminds us that

> Organizing students' stories into categories and themes was a useful process through which to obtain a better understanding of how they view the world. Yet at the same time, any findings based on the categories had the potential to imply that they were discrete, generalizable, and objectively true. (p. 15)

Although we have not provided complete stories of all the students who participated in this study, we have tried to give the reader a snapshot of the concerns relative to these students' educational experiences. The literature supports many of the stories cited in the text; and, from our collective personal experiences as faculty, administrators, and staff, we are cognizant of the host of adjustment problems suffered by students of color on predominantly White campuses.

An overview of the seven institutions selected for this study is provided in Table 1. Data from the interviews are depicted on a conceptually clustered matrix, subsequently discussed, and summarized.

Categories

The coding procedures highlighted in the proceeding section list six categories, each used as a framework to report the findings of this study. These categories are: What you see is what you get (reality of campus culture); Ask anyone—they'll tell you (perceptions of campus and its mission); So, where's the professor? (lack of diversity in professors); If I can make it there, I can make it anywhere (coping statements and self-beliefs); R-e-s-p-e-c-t: Find out what it means to me (campus perceptions of students); and If this world were mine . . . (involvement, future views of self). A display is used to depict the salient information provided by each participant in the case study as it is related to each category. According to Miles and Huberman (1994), a display is a visual format that presents information systematically, so the user can draw valid conclusions and take needed action.

The conceptually clustered matrix, rather than relying on time or role as the organizing principle, orders the display by concepts or variables (Miles and Huberman, 1994). Table 1 depicts the conceptually clustered matrix for the seven institutions. The matrix displays the six strongest themes identified along the first row of the grid and the names of the respective colleges along the first column. According to Miles and Huberman (1994), "Reading across the rows gives the analyst a thumbnail profile of each informant and provides an initial test of the relationship between responses to the different questions. Reading down the columns uses the tactic of making comparisons between the motives of different actors" (p. 129).

Using the statements reported in the matrix, we made numerous observations from the perspective of the participants. The sections within Table 1 provide a discussion of each category and a summary of the responses provided by various participants at the respective institutions as they relate to the guiding research questions. Quotations from the interviews provide depth to the respondents expressed feelings.

Table 1

Conceptually Clustered Matrix: Seven-Institution Survey

	Categories					
PARTICIPANTS	Chapter 4 *What you see is what you get.*	Chapter 5 *Ask anyone— they'll tell you.*	Chapter 5 *R-e-s-p-e-c-t: Find out what it means to me.*	Chapter 4 *So, where's the professor?*	Chapter 5 *If I can make it there, I can make it anywhere.*	Chapter 6 *If this world were mine . . . .*
Balsam College	"I feel that Balsam may lump all the multicultural together and say look how diverse we are . . . by lumping it altogether it looked bigger, but when you looked at it, that was one thing about misrepresentation that I did not like."	"Sometimes I feel like my opinion is always going to be the Black opinion when I'm in class . . . when you're automatically elected Black or White, they assume you know everything about your race.	"I'd rather have a Ku Klux Klan member up in that class tell me how he feels about me than to have someone say, 'Oh, I like you,' and then if you meet them in a dark alley—shoot me."	"In dealing with race issues, we talk about issues, but we don't really get into them."	"Coming here and having not too many people like me was like it helped me reevaluate what I think and what I feel about certain issues and all in all decide how I feel about this campus. It made me a stronger person."	"I don't think we should feel that way, that we're a commodity. I think we should feel like we're people and we're here and we came to Balsam and it was our decision."

48

Cedar University	"... I feel I was lied to and deceived before getting here because they tell you all this lovely stuff in the handbook and then they call your house and explain this and then when you get here it's totally different."	"We talk about certain issues and then when issues of race come up, and you're the only Black person in your class, it's sort of like you have to be the representative and even the teachers look at you to be that way."	"That's what Cedar does a lot of, diversity workshops, but after a while it seems very superficial."	"I really appreciate the fact that the faculty, professors, and administrators make themselves available to students."	"It awakens you to the real world . . . hardships make you stronger and tougher and you can better deal with the real world after Cedar."	"It's a collective we . . . we the students, but also we the administration and faculty. It has to be, if the president is going to put in his catalogue that this is a diverse place and we are so concerned about X, Y, and Z, I need to see. . . . for me actions speak a lot louder than words."
Elm College	"... I'm also upset with the fact that Elm represents itself to be so culturally diverse and so much like a Mecca of races and so forth and you come here and it's not like that."	". . . there are no minority students or professors in the major I selected. Going to classes and discussing books or whatever when they have inklings about race and not wanting to say anything because I don't want to be the voice. . ."	"I think for minority students at Elm, when you come here there's something about yourself that you always have to give up because there is this collective interest that Elm wants everybody to have."	"So for me there was never a sense of failing as far as grades but more of a sense of failing as far as acceptance from the professors in the department."	"With the students here it's [racism] really upsetting. Is the real world like this? Is Elm the real world concentrated or the real racist world?"	"They [Elm administration] just separate us a lot more than you know and then when we get together for a small period of time, they think we're unified and that's only for a week; then the other 28–29 weeks everybody had been off doing their own thing."

(continued)

Table 1 (continued)

				Categories		
PARTICIPANTS	Chapter 4 *What you see is what you get.*	Chapter 5 *Ask anyone—they'll tell you.*	Chapter 5 *R-e-s-p-e-c-t: Find out what it means to me.*	Chapter 4 *So, where's the professor?*	Chapter 5 *If I can make it there, I can make it anywhere.*	Chapter 6 *If this world were mine . . .*
Hickory College	"Hickory 'talks the talk,' they don't 'walk the walk.' This multicultural thing to them is a big game. That's just a word to them. It's a façade."	"When we were talking about Martin Luther King in my F.P. class, they turned to me like I was the expert and I told them I can't talk for all Black people, I'm one Black person from one part of the Black experience. . ."	"I feel that I'm always on trial, somebody is always looking at me and judging me . . . you feel that you have to prove something to them."	". . . they (the faculty) expect you to establish a personal relationship with them, so you have to go talk to them."	". . . it makes you a stronger person, and that is a key positive thing because in the real world, let's face it, you will be facing racism whether you like it or not . . ."	"I never used to really question the system, I would say it was me, I have the problem, but it's not me, it's the system, and I'm not afraid now."
Pine College	"Well, outside the classroom, I try to tell students who are interested in coming here that they want a social life to pop out at them, that this is not the school and you may have to make your own fun here and that's one of the first questions students ask."	"I think that the institution provides a good atmosphere for providing intellectual conversations concerning multiculturalism and diversity, but I feel that oftentimes they fail at certain aspects. For instance, when I came I wanted to see Latino professors and there is only one Latino professor on tenure. . ."	"I think that one positive experience on a political level was a walk-out that we had on Proposition 187. . . . There were a lot of administrators, a lot of professors, a lot of the professors encouraged it, and a lot of the students that I didn't think would be involved in it . . . I really felt powerful . . ."	"You feel like the professors are here for you to learn to make this worthwhile, not just spending $26,000 to be a number. They actually care. I've gone out with the professors, we've just hung out."	"This may sound cocky for me to say, but I believe because of all my other leadership opportunities and experiences here at Pine, I will be successful in whatever I do."	"The first thing I would export to another campus would be our ability to create good programs . . . Get the dialogue going having good facilitators and if the students are the ones facilitating, have the ability to do that."

Redwood College	"I feel like they act like they're so diverse and multicultural . . . This is not a representation of how it is for people who go here."	"I can't oppress myself . . . I want to appreciate all the parts of all ethnicities and not have to choose one side, which I feel like a lot of the times . . . they want you to do that."	". . . I sometimes feel like a token minority. I get put into this group. I'm associated with this group and they don't look at me as an individual."	"You can even find professors at social functions and at committee meetings, or whatever you're doing, you see professors there willing to work for you."	"I have grown a lot just being open-minded, being assertive, getting to know people, looking beyond the surface of things, thinking critically about things that are around me . . . I hope to carry this education both inside and outside the classroom, I hope to carry it throughout my whole life and my job."	"I would say that some of the cons are that you want to see people of color and even though we have people of color here, they won't necessarily see your viewpoints."
Sycamore University	"I think Sycamore is what you make of it, and along the same lines they give you the opportunities. . . ."	. . . a particular student made comments along the lines of, "my mother is Ecuadorian and my father is Scottish," and a fellow student responded to him by a saying "I know it's because your mom is from Ecuador that you have to work harder here than I have to and you can't write as well as me . . ."	"I think more than other institutions that I've studied at, and I've studied at a couple of colleges over the summer, this institution tries to have specific cultural events."	"I know of several occasions, if it weren't for several faculty of color, I don't know how I would have made it from one day to the next."	"I think that [involvement in student activities] has been very empowering to be able to take part in a group or even create something. It has also allowed you to be a leader for yourself and be a part of a team also. I think that's one of the best things about Sycamore."	"If you really wanted to do something to help students of color, sponsor things, student leaders of color going off on a retreat . . ."

4

REALITY
OF CAMPUS CULTURE

What you see is what you get.

Responses to the reality of campus culture were similar across respondents at each of the participating institutions. Many students expressed their enthusiasm concerning their institution's initial display of diversity and multiculturalism in the recruitment process, but then their subsequent disappointment with the reality of the monocultural campuses they found after enrolling at the institution. Responses ranged from tempered disappointment to indignant disapproval. The first column in the conceptually clustered matrix reveals student comments at each of the institutions. According to a student attending Cedar University, "I feel I was lied to and deceived before getting here because they tell you all this lovely stuff in the handbook and then they call your house and explain this and then when you get here it's totally different."

A student attending Hickory College reported, "First of all, when I was applying to Hickory, I had a lot of pitching done to me, they really sold it to me. They waved a lot of banners around saying we're this, we're that, we have this, we have that and I should have noticed right off that it was fishy, that they had to sell it so hard."

Additionally, an Elm College student stated, "I think that I could really say it's definitely a struggle between being honest and still wanting to promote Elm, because as many of us know those are two different things. My opportunities in talking to prospectives (prospective students), I am honest, I try to tell them my honest experience. There's always going to be good and bad with every situation and I've always been one to highlight the good but not forget the bad. This is not going to be the Utopia that we all wish for."

Admission, Recruiting, and Adjustment Concerns

Students at all institutions included in the study questioned the various administrators' motives for recruiting students. Students shared some of their thoughts regarding admission requirements, recruitment strategies, and orientation at their colleges. Many of them expressed their knowledge concerning the institutions' practices to attract minority applicants. Comments included,

> How in the heck do you get people out here without really catering to them and saying we really want you here and we'll do anything to get you here?

> There's a lot of conversation now about how this institution is promoting itself to be diverse but as far as support from the administration and faculty or whatever, as far as culture, it's not what I found to be.

> Those people [recruiters] were the reason most of us are here and the college didn't really take care of us. So once they [recruiters] left, all that potential just disappeared . . .

they're so understaffed in that area [recruiting] there's just not a lot of students coming in, plus the ones that visit see how it is, our feelings and things, so they don't want to deal with that.

The people at the admissions office, registrars office, whatever, they give you a shaded view. They give you the view that they want to present to you that everything is wonderful, when you come here we'll give you money to come and we'll do anything to help you out while you're here and then that's not what really happens.

In the midst of institutions' excitement and commitment to create multicultural environments, some colleges appear to mislead many students. Some students go on to explain their experiences.

My college talks the talk, they don't walk the walk. This multicultural thing to them is a big game. That's just a word to them. It's a façade.

If you go to the admissions office, they'll tell you that this institution is the most wonderful place in the world. That's why half of us are here it's because they suckered us in here, that's exactly what they did. That's one reason why I don't do the admissions thing now is because I just can't sit up there and say "yes come to this institution" in good faith. If prospective students ask me, I would tell them "look brother, don't come. You'll hate this place, because I hate this place. Here let me tell you why, there ain't nothing to do, ain't no support system. The only support system that you have is to play tic-tac-toe with your buddies all day.

I would tell students if you want to come, I still do this with people who are prospectives who are always coming in here, I say if you want to come for an education—great; but if you want to come for a social life—you may want to reconsider.

I had to make a decision whether or not to lie to this woman. To tell her that there's a community, and show her the three people on campus who are Latino; or do I tell her that there's problems, we're a very small community, and we need you cause we need to get bigger and then maybe we'll start to recruit. I had to go through and say that we are a small number of people, and we don't have any classes that are developed toward a Latino Studies major, there's no political movements on campus, there's no organizations, there's nothing. That was very difficult to say.

When I came to this institution, I was led to believe that the classes would be small and the teachers would give you that individual attention because I knew I was going to a predominantly White school and I would need that . . . understanding about my strengths and weaknesses.

Other students struggled with the idea of staying at their institution to make it better for new incoming students. Many expressed their need to take part in creating a solution to make the campus environment a welcoming place for all students, especially students of color.

It's the sense that it's hard to stay here, but the reason why I didn't transfer when I first got here and freaked out, was because I thought I was different so this place needs me. I decided to become the proverbial wart on the nose of academia. I've always been there to make their little picket fence look ugly and spotted in my own little ways.

Yet other students take the approach that if the institution is going to use them, then they are going to utilize the resources of the institution to their advantage also. One student says,

If that's [minority status] what is going to get me into a good grad school, well then sure I'm going to take advantage of that and if that's going to get me better financial aid—damn straight I'm going to take advantage of that.

However, it seems, from observing the students' perceptions, that the majority of them are uncomfortable with the notion that they might have been chosen for admission because of race. They just want to prove to their institutions and to their peers that there is more to them than their race. They want to prove that they are smart and talented and have just as much to give and gain from their institutions and a college education as any other student.

> I feel the bottom line is that I'm here, and I think I deserve to be here, but I just want you of the college to know that sure, you may have accepted me for this, but I'm much more than that. That's why I'm here to prove it.

Three more students take a different approach and say,

> I feel like I have to not only do as well as other students, but better in order to somehow prove that I'm supposed to be here. I feel sometimes that people might look at me and say, "Well, the only reason why she got in here is because she's a colored person," but I realize that what I have to do is ignore that and say I deserve to be here and it's really important to be here.

> I can deal with the school for four years because I look at the longer term of what the school could get me after I graduate from here with a degree because it's a big deal. That degree holds a lot of weight.

> I would advise an incoming student to find your support whether it be large or small and hold onto it, appreciate it because as they were saying, you will definitely be challenged and you will definitely be tried. It's always good to have some type of support. Some type of safe haven you can go to and get you through. I definitely encourage finding, whether it be a friend or a faculty member, or someone in administration, find support and appreciate it.

For students of color, there are a lot of obstacles in the pathways of higher education. Perhaps the first person in the family to attend college and a member of a group of people who was disregarded by the society for many years, a student faces a lot of frustrating and painful situations. Students' responses speak to this point:

I feel that I'm always on trial, somebody is always looking at me and judging me. You feel that you have to prove something to them.

White students don't have to participate, they don't have a standard that they have to abide by. They can just be students and just be comfortable.

It is frustrating that we have to fight so hard, that we are always struggling to stay afloat, but it seems White students don't have to struggle like we do just to survive.

White students don't carry the same things through with them as we have to. It's on our back, it's our load.

I have to fight just to survive, and I think that it comes from the fact that my parents did not graduate from college.

It's not like you are here to have a good time and learn. You are here to prove yourself, that you are capable enough to be in higher education. That's got to stop because that's pressure that comes to you not only by the outside influence, but then you start to question yourself and you start putting the pressure on and it gets too much.

I think my institution sees it as you're Black you need to run fast. If your pace isn't fast enough, you got to run even faster and that's beyond a lot of our capabilities so we just don't make it.

Administrators and Advisors

Academic advisors were often mentioned by students as having a very powerful influence over their first year and academic adjustment.

> I personally feel very negative about the academic advisors at this institution. I feel as though the academic advisors that I have, I use them only to sign my registration and that is all I need them for because they are unable to help me with my career plans . . .

> Maybe it could be my own expectations of my advisors, . . . but I think their understanding of the position is that they register us for classes, tell us what we need to take for a major . . . My understanding of an advisor would be to give me more of an understanding of what advantages there are for taking this class, and how it will help my career goal, to help me to identify some of my strengths . . . Maybe my expectations are too high . . .

> I think that maybe they [advisors] have a conflict of interest of what their position is. I once got into an argument with my advisor, but she expects me to do everything, I am doing her job . . . .

> I get free advice but no action. Everybody wants to tell you how to do it, when to do it, what you should be doing, . . . but don't ask them to help you. They just act like you should be able to figure that out for yourself.

> I had to change her (advisor) because she just didn't think I could be a math major. She tried to do everything she could to discourage me. If I asked her questions, I felt like I was stupid or childish.

Adjustment Concerns

Along with the perception of being overlooked on campus, some students feel that their environment is mentally unhealthy and have a hard time attempting to survive academically and socially. Thus, a large part of their struggle to graduate is being spent overcoming these environmental obstacles.

> Coming in as a freshman you don't know who to turn to when you have questions and there is no assigned group or set person that you can go to when you have problems.

These comments can assist in opening a discussion about educational and psychological topics related to minority student success. How do we provide a painless and productive transition for our students when they are moving from high school environments to higher educational systems? Quite often we observe situations where secondary education did not prepare seniors for entrance into higher education. For example:

> I didn't have any support in high school. We didn't have any counselors who did anything to prepare us for college.

> I have no support here, I basically deal with things by myself.

> If you are not a strong person and you don't self-discipline and things like that, you always need somebody to monitor you, you need an authoritative figure, well you are not going to have it.

Some groups of students always need special attention and consideration, particularly underrepresented groups:

> I think that's the problem there is a lack of support here for people of color.

> There is a lack of support here for women too. If you're lucky enough to be a woman of color then you don't have anything, you can't go to anybody on this campus.

The outcome of the adjustment process is connected with the following characteristics: level of person's confidence, individual adaptability, communication skills, openness to new experience, problem-solving skills, and others. Some students take an active position in searching for adaptation strategies. For example:

> You go through those stages, and that's about growing and how you help yourself understand.

> When I have a problem I call my mom and she calls the school . . . so I don't have too many problems because they know she's going to call and make some trouble for somebody.

> I think the best thing that I do for coping is go home when I can . . .

> I'm trying to adapt to everything, and people here are so different than how you'd expect them to be and sure some of them are close minded, but I think a lot of people are open to a lot of things here.

Also, a purposeful activity usually reduces the level of negative effects of any adjustment processes. For example:

> I've been concentrating on what I want to do and what I want to get out of college.

> What keeps me going is my focus on graduating.

> I'm doing it for my parents for the most part. So as much as I might complain about it and bring out the negative aspects of the institution, I'm not leaving without my papers (degree).

> Now I'm focusing a lot on my education since that is what I came here for in the first place and I tend to block out racism.

I can't give it up because I wouldn't get my diploma from an institution that I didn't try and make difference for my people.

Sophomore year, last year, I stayed in my room mostly and cried because the whole year was miserable.

I'm just burnt out on work. You get tired of the work, you go to bed with your book at night and you wake up with your book.

Other students reported that their campus administration was responsive to their needs. Resources were made available to students to support the various organizations in which they were involved and the cultural events they developed. Some students perceived the administrators to be genuinely concerned about their well-being as students.

One student recalled how the president encouraged students to come and talk with him. Students find the open-door policy practiced by administrators to be a positive attribute of their colleges.

Yes, in January I had a meeting with the president, just go in and speak with him because he always encourages us to come and talk to him, and I've been doing it over the last four years. I went in and talked to him and it felt very positive. I was telling him about the fact that I was kind of frightened because I would be coming towards the end of my college experience and I would have to finally go and look for a job. It just felt good talking to him because he told me that if I needed a recommendation or anything to come by his office, and he would be happy to help me. It made me feel really glad that somebody of his stature would be behind me that way and encourage me to tell him if there was anything he could do to help, just let him know.

I think, there are student organizations on campus for students of color, and I think the university has been overall supportive of those student organizations.

This institution definitely is a place you can network and it's because of the limited number of African American professors on this campus, they do look out for you as far as getting you connected with alumni from and the people that they know in other grad schools.

Yet, some voices of students speak of distrust of the institution and its agents. Distrust presents an unhealthy environment in which students must attempt to survive academically and socially. Thus, a major part of their struggle to graduate is spent trying to overcome these environmental obstacles. In addition to recruitment initiatives and distrust issues with the institutions, students expressed concerns of adjustment to the campus environment and low levels of support.

You don't have the support you had, it almost makes me want to go back to high school as bad as it sounds.

I expected more of my particular race on this campus, not necessarily Latino but Mexicans and I came here and there are no Mexicans here. Another thing I would like to say is that most students from prep schools have larger possibility of having a friend come in with you from the same school. I think from public school, I was one of the two people and every year one or two people get accepted here from my old high school and not all decided to come here anyway so it's a totally different vibe.

Students voiced concerns about racism and the way students of color were being treated on campus. One student summed it up this way:

They have messed up one time. Then they were kicked off campus. All kinds of White people here smoke pot, and they hardly ever get into trouble, they hardly ever get caught. Last year, as far as the Mexicans on campus, there was an issue where a few of the guys got caught smoking pot on campus and right away they were put on probation.

That was a big issue. A few of the deans had a big talk with some of the students. They were talking about the way we dressed and how we intimidated White students on campus, because of our clothes and gang attire. They didn't smile at you, but told us to go around campus introduce ourselves, saying Hi and stuff, my name is so and so, don't be afraid of me. It was ridiculous.

Summary

The expectations and preconceived notions of students of color about their college agents, peers, and campus environment are not in sync with their experienced reality. Most students of color did not think racism would be a problem in college. Fleming's (1984) classic study of more than fifteen years ago revealed a similar finding about Black students.

Unfortunately, faculty and administrators continue to build syllabi, programs, and services based upon inaccurate data and assumptions of who students are and how they learn. The idea of promoting college student development while maintaining the academic integrity of the institution is a formidable task. An essential precondition for success in this process is to provide a supportive, encouraging learning environment that is open, safe, and psychologically positive. With much of the ambiguity surrounding the role and responsibility of faculty and administrators regarding student learning, it is important for the academic community to work together. To better assist students in their learning, creative leadership is needed from student affairs professionals in working with secondary organizations, families, academic affairs, community colleges, and community agencies.

A great deal of the dialogue and statements in this text reveal that the college experiences of minority students at predominantly White institutions require a lot of effort beyond that of their White counterparts. Minority students state that due to their perception of a weak K–12 educational experience, they must retool themselves and catch up so as to compete with their nonminority peers.

Hurn (1993) and Bourdieu and Passeron (1977) view education as an important social and political force in the process of class reproduction. By appearing to be an impartial and neutral "transmitter" of the benefits of a valued culture, schools are able to promote inequality in the name of fairness and objectivity. In more specific terms, a child is influenced by his or her family social values and status that are often influenced by the level of education attained by the child's parents.

This issue is important for minority students. Many institutions and professionals in higher education continue to view standardized tests as the strongest indicator of success and assume that students of color, who often receive lower scores, are not capable of achieving.

The decline in the quality of an individual's K–12 educational experience is often exacerbated by the fact that far too many students have not been properly trained in public school and are unable to understand the process within higher education in order to take full advantage of the system. Exposure to college life only teaches some minority students the full extent of their own inadequacies that impede their success.

In no way are the researchers implying that nonminority students do not face similar issues; however, we do believe that students of color experience their collegial environments in ways unlike their majority peers, ways that often stem from unequal treatment. Formulating new and creative methods to make campuses welcoming environments is indeed a challenge (Stage and Manning, 1992). The assumption is that the college campus is a place where people from various backgrounds come together for a common goal, to learn. While learning, however, students try to find others with whom they share similar backgrounds and experiences. Students also try to find places and objects that remind them of who they are and who they desire to become.

The issues articulated by students in the transcripts speak to the ever-increasing need to assess college and university campus climate. Campus climate is a collage of the interpersonal and group dynamics that comprise the experience of participants in a collegiate setting (Edgert, 1994). The pictures the various institutions painted were perceived by the students as unfair representations of

the campus environments they encountered during their matriculation. According to Edgert, a better understanding of campus climate is crucial to enhancing campus diversity initiatives.

An important lesson to be gleaned from the responses provided
by the students is that colleges and universities must clearly articulate
and provide an accurate account of campus diversity initiatives and
profiles. Every institution wants to put its best foot forward in marketing and promotion, yet they must concern themselves with providing an accurate depiction of what the consumer (e.g., student,
parent, external constituent) will get in return for his or her investment. If this investment is predicated upon a setting that not only
facilitates but also extols the values of diversity and multiculturalism,
then this should be reported, but reported in a manner that accurately reflects the current status of these initiatives on the campus.

Research has demonstrated the importance of establishing a
network of diversity to provide students of color with the support
necessary to successfully complete their chosen academic programs, simultaneously addressing their needs for social and emotional wellness. Nettles et al. posited in *Comparative and Predictive Analyses of Black and White Students' College Achievement
and Experiences,* among the most important findings highlighted,
the importance of the student-environment fit as measured by students' feelings that the university is nondiscriminatory.

Again, student environment and the requisite effect on campus
climate play a significant role in academic success for all students,
particularly minority students. If institutions are to promote diversity and multiculturalism, then they must be truthful regarding the
current multicultural status of their institutions. Future projections
and altruistic intentions are acceptable, but they do not replace the
honest portrayal of the institution's stance on these initiatives.
Often, projections and intentions combined with an initial display
of diversity shade the true campus climate. This in turn leads to
student dissatisfaction with not only the issue of campus diversity,
but also the overall issue of institutional integrity. As one Elm student replied, " . . . I am also upset with the fact that Elm represents itself to be so culturally diverse and so much like a Mecca of
races and so forth and you come here and it's not like that."

5

THE LACK
OF MULTICULTURALISM
AND HOW IT AFFECTS
STUDENTS

Ask anyone—they'll tell you . . .

Minority students often lament their role as spokesperson for their racial and ethnic groups, a role they are invariably expected to play in predominantly nonminority settings. The statements in the matrix uncover several instances in which these students have felt the need to speak in general terms about their cultural or ethnic groups and in specific terms about their individual experiences as members of these groups in various settings.

A Balsam College respondent reported, "Sometimes I feel like my opinion is always going to be the Black opinion." A Hickory College student posited, "When we were talking about Martin Luther King in my F. P. class, they turned to me like I was the expert and I told them I can't talk for all Black people." Similarly, a Redwood College student responded, "I can't oppress myself . . . I want to appreciate all the parts of all ethnicities (a triracial student)

and not have to choose one side, which I feel like a lot of the times
. . . they want you to do that."

The experiences articulated by students were common across
the interview data. The matrix only captures a narrow cross section of their many responses recapitulating the same theme—
minority students feeling the need to speak for their entire race.
Most respondents readily reported their dislike for the precarious
position this role of spokesperson connotes on a majority campus. Yet, many acknowledged and accepted this role as a *fete
accompli,* as initial exposure to a role they would be required to
play in many future contexts outside of the academic setting.

Several students implied that their dual role as a minority student and a college student significantly impacted their identity
and development. These students exhibited what many have
termed a "double consciousness," a strategy used to successfully
matriculate within their academic and cultural communities (Roebuck and Murty, 1993). While they gain a better understanding
of their identity development as college students, they must also
seek clarity in their development as *minority* college students.
These two competing measures of identity development manifest
themselves in the students' daily interactions inside and outside of
the classroom.

In many of the interviews, students expressed their desire for
their peers to become fired up about racial issues without worry-
ing about offending campus constituents. These students
expressed a desire for their peers to be honest when discussing
issues of race. Students commented that when discussions of race
occurred on campus, they seldom got to the heart of what was
really happening. One student attributed the lack of sincere dialogue to the misunderstanding of cultural difference.

Students stated that they did not get into discussions about
race in class because they were afraid of saying something offensive or that they would become emotionally charged. Students did
comment, however, that when they had discussions with close
friends about race, the discussions were much calmer and more
honest than their classroom experiences.

Throughout the interview, all the students seemed to place a huge value on open, honest discussion of racial issues. They felt this type of openness was what brought the minority community as well as the entire campus together.

Another topic uncovered in the interview was the idea that students felt they were viewed as the spokesperson for their ethnic groups. In other words, they felt that they were asked for the opinion of the minority groups and not for their personal opinions. Students were very vocal about this issue.

> Sometimes I felt like my opinion is always going to be the Black opinion when I'm in class . . . when you're automatically elected Black or White, they assume you know everything about your race.

> We talk about certain issues and then when issues of race come up, and you're the only Black person in your class, it's sort of like you have to be the representative and even the teachers look at you to be that way.

> I think one thing that I want to say is that sometimes you have to represent your whole entire race. For me that's such a big thing because I am a token Native American on campus and I have professors, students, administrators look to me to represent my entire race.

A related theme to the individual viewed as the spokesperson for an entire group was the notion that students often believed they were not seen as individuals, but as generic parts of a larger group. Students were concerned about their assigned responsibilities as spokespersons for their respective minority community and for their race. Students believed assumptions were often made about them based on their minority group membership. They also had qualms about their institutions' proclivities for lumping all minority students into categories.

I find myself being the only person of color in my class and I always feel like I'm on trial whether it's talking about one aspect or another, but people assume that because I am a person of color that I can have the answers for everything and that gets very tiring.

I don't know everything there is to know about Africa. I was supposed to be the spokesperson for all Black people, and I just didn't want to be that person.

There is no place to be yourself, you can't speak for yourself without speaking for your whole community. That's something that college needs to account for, and administration and the faculty and everybody else.

R-E-S-P-E-C-T: Find Out What It Means to Me
Campus Perceptions of Students

Past research on the minority student's experience on predominantly White campuses reveals the tenuous relationships the minority student often maintains with fellow nonminority administrators, faculty, peers, and staff. An array of potential causes can be attributed to these strained associations, including lack of a critical mass of minority students, harassment based on ethnic identification, curricula that imply assimilation as the only measure of success, low expectations from professors, social events and hangouts that are off limits, and negative attitudes from labeling and placement.

Collectively or individually, each cause contributes to the minority student's collegiate experience. A number of these experiences are reflected in the comments the respondents provided in the conceptually clustered matrix. A Cedar University student responded, "That's what Cedar does a lot of, diversity workshops, but after a while it seems very superficial." An Elm College student advanced, "I think for minority students at Elm, when you come here there's something about yourself that you always have to give up because there is this collective interest that Elm wants everybody to have." Additionally, a Sycamore University student commented, "I think more than other institutions that I've studied at, and I've studied at a couple of colleges over the summer, this institution tries to have specific cultural events."

A common thread throughout the respondents' statements was the importance of being recognized and respected as a minority student on campus, a respect they often perceived to be missing in the higher education setting. According to Roebuck and Murty (1993), "the literature on Black students attending White schools documents campus problems involving interpersonal relationships, personal identity, and Black consciousness." The problems uncovered in the literature are also indicative of the experience of other minority populations on majority campuses. It is the minority student who faces racial slights, feelings of alienation, and discriminatory practices on the American college campus.

To create campus environments that promote a sense of respect for all student populations, institutions must employ broad-based initiatives that address the interests, motivations, and nuances indigenous to each cultural and ethnic group. The academy must concentrate on institution-wide transformation and avoid the traditional individual transformation tactics typically employed (Gordon and Strode, 1992).

The comments provided in this category reveal the students' attitudes and feelings regarding the level of respect they perceive is afforded to them by their respective institutions with regard to their individual cultural and ethnic differences. Noteworthy, across interview data, is the pervasive belief that by emphasizing cultural and ethnic differences, many institutions have become indifferent and even suspect of their student's abilities, viewing them all from a position of substandard achievement potential. If institutions do not work to transform these ideas and notions on a more holistic scale, minority students will continue to feel the need to go beyond the normal call of duty to demonstrate their ability to meet the very basic qualifications necessary to succeed within the academy. A Hickory College student provides an excellent summation of this point: "I feel that I'm always on trial, somebody is always looking at me and judging me . . . you feel that you have to prove something to them."

So, Where's the Professor?
Lack of Diversity in Professors

The collegiate student's experience in a higher educational setting is greatly influenced by a number of variables, both cognitive and noncognitive. These variables include academic preparation, background experiences, socialization processes, and relationships with faculty. Although a number of these variables work in tandem to produce what is noted as the collegiate experience, it is the influence of one particular variable that has been cited as the most central component in ensuring the student's successful matriculation—establishing a relationship with faculty.

The lack of students or faculty of color seems to affect some students greatly.

> One big type of covert racism that exists on this campus is the lack of professors of color. I think that's been very unfortunate for me because I feel that it's nice to be able to talk to a professor of color who might have a common interest that we might be able to share.

> I was a computer science major and I was the only woman in the whole department and, of course, I was the only minority, and people sat me down and treated me like I was a little kid, totally patronized me, because it was a man's field.

> You're not able to focus on the situation at hand, when you are at a predominantly White campus, with not many outlets, and with many prejudiced professors.

I came in and there was a lot of times we'd be in biology labs, and I'd ask questions and give answers. They wouldn't be acknowledged until someone else gave that same answer. Those are things that for one have never happened to me until now.

I think there is also pressure that we add onto ourselves. I take a lot of science classes and I'm really the only Black person in the whole class and I feel that I have to do well or people think that all Black people are doing bad. It's an extra burden because I'm representing not just myself but others.

The lack of minorities on this campus, like I hate going to class and being the only person of color in the room.

For instance in the classroom a lot of the time I'm the only African American in the class and more than that I'm the only Black male in there.

Sometimes the omission of racial or ethnic groups from discussions or issues helps ignite racial tensions. Other times, students of color seemed to feel undue pressure to speak up for their racial or ethnic group, especially if they felt members of other groups were likely to do so, if they did not.

There are no minority students or professors in the major that I selected—human development. Going to classes and discussing books, or whatever when they have inklings about race and not wanting to say anything because I don't want to be the voice. But then getting so disgusted with the fact that a bunch of White people are talking about a Black person's experience or a person of color's personal experience, just weighing that and getting so frustrated that I want to leave, or I want to cry or just scream at everybody.

I wanted to be an art major for a short period of time when I came to my institution. I encountered people in the department who were not at all thinking about the best interest of the students, and those people made it impossible for me to proceed in education or even as a secondary interest here.

I find myself now discouraged about chemistry because of the lack of support. I don't know if I would be one to encourage others coming in after me to be a part of it just because of my experience, and I think it had a lot to do with being the only African American—just point blank. So for me, there was never a sense of failing as far as grades but more of a sense of failing as far as acceptance from the professors in the chemistry department. It was more like I had to smile a little bit bigger or converse a little bit more in order to get that acceptance from the professor, and in that sense there was a fear of, because I'm different, will they like me for who I am. That's been a struggle and fear for four years.

Some students spoke very passionately about the commitment of the faculty to support them in class and out of class at the institutions in the study.

At the beginning of this term, I had some serious, serious problems with my car and I needed to get a lot of money to get my car fixed, something like $600. There was no way for me to get that money for a loan or anything, and one faculty informed me about student affairs and they worked out some things for me and they were able to get my car fixed because I have a job here in town. I needed my car so it was a necessity and they came through for me and helped me out.

I'd say about seven professors, three African American and four White professors, came through for me and helped me to get everything that I needed to get done and helped me slip through some loopholes here and there. I got a lot of support from the general body of students because I've been here so long a lot of them know me, and my situation, so that little extra piece of motivation was what I needed to get through a tough time.

One student told a story of support about trying to make a decision to transfer to another institution. He received both positive and negative support from faculty and administrators.

I've had positive things happen like with professors trying to help me while I was trying to transfer. There were only two professors that I talked to, administrative people, registrars, and all of that good stuff, they were the only two people who actually said you can make a decision for yourself, you decide if you're going to fill out applications, make sure that you're determined. They helped me make my decisions, the others tried to persuade me to stay within this university and try to make something of it. At the time I was thinking about transferring, I shouldn't have to work that much harder to stay here when something that was promised to me, that's the university's fault. If one more person tried to persuade me to stay here, I would have been outraged. When I'm telling you that this has been my life's dream, and I can't work in that environment and you keep telling me to stay there in spite of it. I don't have to. I don't think that's a good representation of the university, or what the university is supposed to do which is to help you obtain your goals.

What is alarming are the various accounts of prejudices on the part of the faculty, both in and out of the classroom. These instances are likely to impact and influence the students involved, particularly as these same faculty are supposed to serve as role models, mentors, and academic leaders on campus. Nevertheless, students describe several instances of racist attitudes and stereotyping.

I've had a professor, my advisor, who told me, you'll never make it as an engineer, you need to go to a different department and do something else for the rest of your life because you'll never make it.

I had a professor ask me, "What is a Black girl from Detroit doing in an economics class?" That to me is just not what I expected from an institution like this. I had the same professor ask me, "Do you ever wonder if you're here because of affirmative action?

Coming in as a freshman, you don't know who to turn to when you have questions and there's no set group or set person that you can go to when you have problems. You have to go and feel your way around. Here I am still, about to be a sophomore next year and I still don't have a faculty person that I know that I can talk to when I have problems.

One student's story about an award she received that she wasn't sure she deserved, summarizes the overall group's feeling that faculty and administration held lesser expectations for the group, due to their racial or ethnic identity.

I had a weird thing happen to me when I was a sophomore. I was about to declare my English major, and I hadn't declared my major yet, but I was about to, and my advisor knew I was going to. I made good grades; good enough to keep my scholarship but not perfect and the English department awarded me the (prestigious departmental) prize for the most promising new English major. Then I talked to my friends, who are in the same major with better grades than me. So why did I get handpicked for this award? I don't want to think about why you would pick a Puerto Rican English major over an Anglo blonde English major, maybe I actually deserved it. I actually deserved being the most promising new English major in my class. Then there was this little voice in my head going, "This is wrong, they know you're poor, they know you need money, they know that you could use a library relief for $150 and you could use the recognition and the self-esteem." It sort of ruined that little cloud of achievement and made it cheap, that underlying suspicion, that fear, that made it disaffirming about the action.

Minority students have problems extending trust to White faculty and administrators because of background differences. Students want faculty members who will understand their cultural uniqueness. More importantly, students want to connect with a faculty member who can empathize with the pressures minority students face on predominantly White campus.

I have only had one Black professor in three years and that's this semester. When you're in the sciences you don't see anyone that looks like you. To me, that makes a big difference. It's tough when you're in the sciences. Sometimes you just want someone to relate to you and who can understand you. You don't see that in the math and sciences. You see that in the sociology department, some in psychology, but sociology mainly.

When I found out last year that there was a Korean professor in chemistry for one year and she had to leave, when I found out physics had a Korean, I felt it makes it more comfortable. I'm used to having White professors. I didn't even notice that biology is not as diverse a faculty but when you think about it, when there is somebody who does look like you it's more comfortable.

I think the administration or faculty, whatever, they see that there is a small group of us here so they always expect us to respond and to give input to everything and it kind of wears you down after a while. Because you're a Black, African American, or international student they look at you and say that you should have something to say all the time about everything because there will only be one or two of you in a class. They kind of make you feel that you're carrying a burden that you should not have to do because the other students that are here don't have to do that. Because if you're going to a class and there are twenty-five White students and two Black students, they could just blend in and the discussion would be okay, okay, okay, and now you Black person what do you have to say?

The faculty will look at you and say this is what you need to do . . . but that's what they want you to do and what they feel you should be doing, but it's not an assessment of what you are capable of doing.

Professor asking a student to share part of one's culture also puts a lot of pressure on you as the artifact, the cultural artifact.

I think for minority students, when they come here, there's something about yourself that you always have to give up because there is this collective interest that this institution wants everybody to have.

Summary

Probably the most significant element influencing the performance level of many students is their inability to connect to an institutional agent. Past research unanimously supports this notion. Even more disturbing is the fact that racialized climates in predominantly White college classrooms are the norm. Pouncey (1993) stated that Black students reported they are assumed to represent the "Black" point of view as if it were monolithic; as if there were such a thing. Subsequently, minority students are left feeling alienated and isolated due to these inhospitable practices.

It would be an uncommon incident for a faculty member to ask an American of European descent about the global view of how White people relate to a specific topic or how they themselves experience a particular situation. The academic community would totally shun this form of questioning. Yet this is what is often asked of students of color.

Because the classroom may be the one place that sets the tone for how students make sense of their collegiate experience, one may assume that most students of color are tired of being treated as a collective, rather than as individuals with diverse thoughts, ideas, and perceptions. This particular treatment only trivializes and belittles their existence and experience as unique individuals.

Ironically, students' perceptions suggest that preconceived notions or falsehoods centered around the idea that most of them are *homogenous creatures* that act and think alike sets the stage for White faculty and students to force students of color into collective vexation. Students of color are frustrated and incensed by mainstream presumptions of inferiority and homogeneity, which are notions often formulated before they even set foot on campus.

Faculty members are an extension of the institution; one could even advance the notion that faculty are the institution. Research has revealed that they provide a needed outlet, a support system for students, especially minority students, one that is often missing in majority environments (Allen, 1986).

For minority students on the majority campus, these relationships prove to be even more critical aspects in their educational experiences. For example, a study by Allen (1986) proved that for Black students on predominantly White campuses, relationships with faculty are one of the most effective predictors of student outcomes.

Responses in this category supported the existing research in this area and revealed the importance of student-faculty relationships, ones that many students identified as the primary source of support regarding their continued matriculation. A Cedar University respondent reported, "I really appreciate the fact that the faculty, professors, and administrators make themselves available to students." Similarly, a Hickory College student responded, "They (the faculty) expect you to establish a personal relationship with them, so you have to go talk to them." A Sycamore University student stated, "I know of several occasions, if it weren't for several faculty of color, I don't know how I would have made if from one day to the next."

The importance of creating and fostering relationships between faculty and students should be central to the mission of every institution of higher learning. According to Magolda (1987), students at the highest level of complexity in intellectual development preferred relationships with faculty that emphasized working together as colleagues.

6

COPING: INVOLVEMENT, IDENTITY, AND EDUCATIONAL OUTCOMES

If I can make it there, I can make it anywhere.

Coping Statements and Self-Beliefs

The conceptually clustered matrix captures the various comments made by the student respondents regarding matriculation at their respective institutions and the preparation this process has provided them for life beyond academe. A common refrain cited by these respondents implied that their experiences as minority students on predominantly White campuses in addition to the normal rigors of pursuing an undergraduate education had prepared them for most postmatriculation experiences. Responses provided in the matrix reflect both positive and negative institutional experiences that have molded and shaped students' views concerning life after graduation.

One Elm College student commented, "With the students here it [racism] is really upsetting. Is the real world like this? Is Elm the real world concentrated or the real racist world?" A Pine College student stated, "This may sound cocky for me to say, but I believe because of all my other leadership opportunities and experiences here at Pine, I will be successful in whatever I do." Parallel to this student's comment, a Redwood College student replied, "I have grown a lot just being open-minded, being assertive, getting to know people, looking beyond the surface of things . . . I hope to carry this education both inside and outside the classroom, I hope to carry it throughout my whole life and my job."

The higher education setting becomes a training ground for these students not only for academic development, but also for social development. It is often their adeptness at managing social relationships that proves to be the most salient contributor to their higher education experiences. These very skills of maintaining healthy liaisons with fellow nonminority peers and faculty members, while concomitantly maintaining a healthy identity and sense of self, are prerequisite skills needed for successful matriculation in the world beyond the ivy tower.

The process of making it academically, socially, and psychologically for minority students is an arduous task, and by surviving this experience they prove to themselves that they possess the ability to make it outside the academy. Fleming (1984) asserted that predominantly White colleges had not successfully mitigated issues such as minority student isolation, classroom bias, and perceptions of hostile campus environments.

Student organizations, particularly social and cultural ones, play a significant role for some minority students.

Involvement

Getting involved is one of the most important aspects about college. I would say take advantage of the support services. Take advantage of every opportunity that presents itself. Take advantage of the openness of the faculty and administration. Basically when you do that, you open the doors to more opportunities and other things. I think too often there are some students whether they're minority or other, that get too complacent or are not active enough in terms of their own personal advancement. You have to be active in terms of making things happen for yourself and that might mean taking advantage of things that are there.

I think the more involved you get the more you care about what happens to everything that goes on in this school, the people and everybody. If you're not involved, and involvement doesn't necessarily mean you have to be a president of the student body, but just doing your own thing. Like maybe you're in glee club or maybe an RA or something. Just having a stake in what goes on or having some position that allows you to talk to other people about what's going on that makes you care more about the school itself. Or learning to contribute to the school, especially if your job is a contribution to the school, for instance, being an RA or a mentor, that makes you have a sense of responsibility to the school as opposed to staying in your room and not doing anything but classwork.

I've been involved in a lot of things and the major thing that comes up that I get from it is I can make a difference, I can change things and that makes a big difference to me. I can do something on campus that can really affect things.

One big concern expressed by many of these students was the lack of involvement by other minority students on campus. The students who are not involved have a different view than those who are involved. Some noninvolved students found that existing campus-based student committees often were not accomplishing their goals and did not feel the need to join these organizations to remedy these situations.

However, many of the students interviewed expressed either disinterest or disappointment in these organizations on their campuses, even as they acknowledged the potential value of their existence. For those students who did participate, the significance of these clubs and organizations usually coincided with the students' level of involvement. For others, participating in organizations simply failed to interest them or assist them in overcoming their ill feelings toward their institutions.

Downside of Involvement

I found that if I'm not a participant in the clubs here it's because I find myself wanting to hide because of the misery that I've experienced here. It's just that I don't want to participate in any clubs, I don't want to participate in any discussions, it's very discouraging, my whole experience was in most cases kind of "I don't care" type feelings.

I was going to say that a lot of it comes from apathy also. We try to get students to come out and voice their opinions but they won't come. They say it's not going to change and that's a big problem because students don't want to work to change things. They want to complain and say it's not this and this and we're not getting that, but when it comes time to say what do you want, they just say, "I don't know."

There is a fight that you have to go through when you come to college, especially as a student of color, as a woman, or as someone from the city, or different type of background.

On this campus, I don't think it's designed for us to succeed, I think it's here to break as many of us as possible. I don't think the system is for our benefit, we have to realize that just to get through this the best way we can.

Another student stressed that everyone should be responsible for change.

Regardless of how large the number of students of color is, there still needs to be that level of involvement from everyone because whatever decisions that are made, they are going to affect you, so one needs to be a part of the team to make things happen.

Some of my friends aren't involved in certain organizations and it's interesting to hear their perspectives on how they view it here. For example, oftentimes people who aren't involved and don't really know what the dynamics of the organization are, they think the organization isn't really doing much or that it's not particularly successful. At the same time, when they're making those judgments they don't try to go to meetings or to help out or to even just see for themselves and actually realize the organization is doing things.

I don't think academics is all that makes a school and although the institution has a very high academic standing in the United States, socially it's just in a doghouse, I believe. I think it's geared more towards certain students and this may be intentional, unintentional, who knows.

Other students shared their views of involvement regarding activities that are built around alcohol.

I don't get into the whole drinking scene that is the entire social scene here at Cedar—it's celebrated and caters to one kind of community [White students], and I've never been part of that.

I think that's a valid complaint from most students, well not most students, but students of color that there's nothing to do if you don't drink, if you don't like frats there's nothing to do.

Everything from professors' meeting to student organizations, senior meetings are held at a bar and those who do not drink or who don't feel comfortable around certain people when they drink, it's not good atmosphere.

There is another thing you have to deal with here and that's White people and alcohol.

Everybody gets drunk, that's the only thing to do.

Club-Specific Involvement

Segregation is still a major issue on college campuses and student affairs professionals will need to address this as the student population continues to grow with multicultural students. Students also stressed the need to have a platform where all can come together to work and discuss issues pertaining to campus.

You have your individual groups, don't get me wrong. You have the Korean club, the ABLE Casa Latino, you have all your different groups, but when it comes down to it you need a bigger group that involves everybody collectively because that's where we get into trouble because we're all focused on our own groups. I don't know if the dialogue or the relations between minorities on campus are even that excellent.

The clubs are run by students and they have to feel secure in their groups. I've gone to some clubs and if you go to this club it's all that race, you go to that club and it's all that race. Even themselves, they don't want to intermix.

It's like a lot of activities are very segregated. You might think that everybody can go there and do that, but when you see it, the Black students are over there and the White students are over there and it's a very segregated type of activity. Therefore, it leaves you with very little options.

I've heard that my institution is forty percent minorities and yet, we're very isolated. One of the things I don't like is the reputation. Like why do all the Koreans hang out together? That really just bugs me because it seems like they are saying you guys just want to hang out with your-selves and you don't want to associate with anybody else. I think that overall Koreans get a bad rap here. That's sort of more personal.

Even if involvement sometimes takes the form of expressing dis-content with life on campus, many students expressed a sense of connection to the college and their fellow students. Many within-race issues stood out, one being the idea of minority students accus-ing each other of selling out to the White establishment.

. . .When I came here in my first term, I was talking to someone who was of a different race and instead of get-ting race stuff from Whites I got it from Blacks on campus. I had a lot of people actually talk down to me calling me a sell-out and . . . before we can say we have a problem with the Whites on campus, I think we should first say we have a problem with the Blacks. With the minorities. We have a very big problem that's just not going to go away.

Some students also acknowledged existing problems among students of color on campus.

I think also that there have been a lot of problems within the African American and Latino communities in the larger respect with people of color on the campus. I don't think the unity, and not even just unity, just the basic respect for other individuals is not present. There have been so many, from what I've been told, negative and just downright dirty experiences that have happened among and between peo-ple of color on this campus. Too many people have been so focused and either it's just about them and nothing else can ever get in the way of that, and that's caused a lot of dis-sension and a lack of unity among the people on campus. They're people of color, and then of course if we can't have unity within ourselves, the chain effect, we can't have unity within the rest of the community.

Nationality also plays a role in terms of racism across minority groups. Examples are given of Indian students who negatively view biracial relationships, as well as students of Pakistani and African American descent.

> Growing up as an American, I have very different views from someone who is Pakistani, who's coming here as an international student. By virtue of me being in a relationship with another person of another race, to these people it is totally unacceptable.

> Some international students who are Indian won't speak to me because they find out I'm Pakistani. Even though I'm an American, that's bad enough. I'm Americanized, but by virtue of being Pakistani that's something that I've experienced.

> There's huge racism of what is acceptable behavior and speech; it's like a self-hatred. Even if you're tan, I'm tan right now because I have a really good tan, and other Asian students ask me why are you in the sun, why do you hang out with these darker people, why do you hang out with the gumbies, which is the word for Black people, it's a derogatory word. They [Asians] ask me why do I want to be dark, why don't you use a bleaching powder, why don't you wax.

Each of these scenarios represents examples of prejudices that seem to exist across all nationalities and cultures. There are a variety of ways in which people intentionally or unintentionally participate in practices of prejudice and superiority based on race, gender, intelligence, socioeconomic status, and other factors. It often happens that educational systems and the beliefs of their participants perpetuate such notions as biases, preconceptions, and prejudice.

The students who are biracial express that they believe they exist somewhere between cultures. One student says,

> It's really hard for me to identify with either group when both are rejecting me and accepting me at the same time.

Another student says that she feels she has to separate her friends into two racial categories.

> I have my Caucasian friends and I have my Latino friends, and I feel that I can never combine them, it's like I have to have two separate identities.

These students also feel rejected by people from their own families.

> I've experienced more prejudice from my Chinese side of the family just because I'm a half-breed. I'm a half-White devil.

Other students express that they have been hurt by their families who reject them for wanting to date outside of their race or view them as having become too "Americanized."

> I don't think I can feel extremely comfortable anywhere.

One student responds,

> I'm not really personally comfortable here, and I think it has to do with the fact that I'm still trying to figure out my place.

Another responds,

> Many of the poor people try to play up what they have to relate better to the richer students, but the wealthier students attempt to downplay what they have in order to relate better to the poorer students. I think my institution ignores the class issue a lot and it's a thing that I'd like to talk about more.

Summary

From the students' voices in this study, it is clear that they must be strong, independent, self-starters with well-developed self-concepts and purposes in order to be successful in these predominantly

White institutions. Even minority students who have attained high levels of scholastic success are not immune from the effects of isolation, alienation, and cultural dissonance on predominantly White campuses.

Dorsey and Jackson (1995) conducted a study about students of color and their college experiences. The study revealed that in spite of their level of academic satisfaction and achievement, a substantial percentage of these students reported feelings of sociocultural isolation in terms of the campus environment. Findings indicated:

> Slightly more than half (55%) of the students felt that there was no feeling of shared interests and purposes, nor a strong sense of community on the campus. Almost the same number (50%) reported that services, information, and facilities were not conducive to the success of African American students. In addition, a little over half (53%) of these students reported that the campus atmosphere was not conducive to racial harmony and balance. For example, 62% felt that the universities did not adequately address issues of discrimination and racism. Forty-six percent believed that the university made no effort to make students feel comfortable on campus. Seventy-six point eight percent (76.8%) indicated that it was difficult to meet and make friends. (p. 192)

Hence, this dynamic is not a new or isolated phenomenon. How students of color maintain positive outlooks about their collegiate experiences, in light of these disturbing facts, is a mystery. It is apparent from the students' voices that before most of them can concentrate on academics, they must first feel comfortable in the campus community. Students of color must feel comfortable with the subject matter being taught. Invariably, minority students deal with issues that most White students are not cognizant of, but this lack of cognizance must be addressed if we are to ensure these students' success.

Paul (1998), in her investigation of African American males, found that their expectations regarding future life success were deeply rooted in their individual experiences within nonminority contexts. The minority individual who has matriculated in non-minority contexts develops a much clearer view of how institutional racism and oppression can thwart personal success. Institutions must determine if they are comfortable with being identified as crucibles for combining elements of bias and racism in the name of preparation for future life challenges.

If This World Were Mine
Involvement, Future Views of Self

The final category captures the respondents' views of the perfect institutional environment. An institutional environment can be studied from a number of different perspectives—physical, human aggregate, organizational, and perceptual (Moos, 1985). The comments provided by the respondents overwhelmingly uncovered their notions of the ideal institutional environment from a minority student's viewpoint, one that is often at odds with many traditional institutional environments.

A Balsam College student commented on the necessity of changing the perceptions of individuals within the institution regarding the role of diversity and diversity initiatives geared toward attracting more minority students. The respondent's view of the current institutional climate is reflected as, "I don't think we should feel that way, that we're a commodity. I think we should feel like we're people and we're here and we came to Balsam and it was our decision."

A Pine College student commented on the importance of implementing effective programming to not only garner minority students' interest, but also to educate the institution as a whole on issues impacting these student populations. The student responded, "The first thing I would export to another campus would be our ability to create good programs . . . Get the dialogue going having

[sic] good facilitators and if the students are the ones facilitating, have the ability to do that." Similarly, a Sycamore University student replied, "If you really want to do something to help students of color, sponsor things, student leaders of color going off on a retreat. . . ."

Creating campus environments that are conducive to student attraction, satisfaction, and stability requires a certain synergistic effort on the part of student populations and campus officials (Gordon and Strode, 1992). An ideal campus environment for the minority student, as reported by several respondents, is a place where the individual feels a sense of "cultural comfort"—where all facets of the campus community recognize and value their contributions as individuals. Functional accouterments are translated into symbolic gestures of goodwill and altruistic intentions. Ingle (1994) informs us that the challenge of diversity is inescapable and every institution will eventually face it. Understanding the significance of campus climate and how to systematically assessment it is a critical step in meeting that challenge.

Students also identified many positive experiences of their exposure to cultural diversity on campuses and in the classroom. The students expressed joy in talking and learning about other cultures during their college experience.

I've met a bunch of people from a bunch of different places and that's been the most positive thing.

I would say I met a lot of people here from other countries which I thought was neat. I wouldn't have learned much about . . . culture which I thought is something I found I'm really interested in.

I've found being here in the community of the women of color has been something neat that I never had in high school, and I don't know if I would have that in a lot of other places that I would go to. The women I know here I really like a lot and I've been lucky.

I found in my four years of college that you must be politically correct. If you're not at that level and there's a situation and you don't respond to it in the P.C. way that's
expected, then there's something wrong with you; you're
militant, you're angry, and you have a problem. The one
thing that I've found is that they are (White students) P.C.
but they are not being honest with me . . . I don't care
how politically correct you are, if you're not being honest,
then what's the value of what you have to say? It really
amazes me how I can come here and have other students
preaching at me about their political perspective and making me feel strange for doing things I've always done, and
that I just see as normal. Because their causes and their
views are right and it's almost as if they're so P.C. that they
go from being all-accepting to very limiting, it gets very
limiting to other people and that really bothers me a lot.

I don't feel that I should have to control who I am when
my emotions run wild. I think that's important for this
question because I think people feel that when I get loud
or when I get angry that it's a bad sign, but we're showing
that we have true emotions, but I think that's what we
hide when we're here on these campuses is our true emotions, we keep a lot of things bottled inside, and I don't
think that's good. If other people are angry or offended
they have no problems saying it, so I think it's good for us
to be vocal with our emotions.

It awakens you to the real world. Hardships make you
stronger and tougher and you can better deal with the real
world after college.

I think it prepared me for what I'm supposed to do when
I get out of here . . . It's taught me where people stand
and to accept the reality that there is ignorance outside in

the real world and that's an obstacle that we are all going to face outside of college and that these obstacle are a preparation for the world.

I feel that my experience has taught me to be sure of who I am. I think they built a stronger character in me in terms of preparing me for the future and what I choose. I think it's made me a stronger person.

I would say that one of the pros is that it makes you stronger. It makes you much more confident and resourceful in order to get anything done, get anything for yourself, get anything that makes you happy you have to learn to stand strong for yourself.

The students agreed that their most positive experiences were those related to their involvement on campus. Some identified the people they have met and the experiences they have shared as being one of these positives.

The most positive experience for me, one of the things has been the people that I've met this first year. I'm a freshman. I've grown close to a lot of them and they make me feel comfortable.

I think that people should not be afraid to say things. It really helps when people get to know each other.

The pro is finding strength within yourself.

It's a struggle, but that's how you grow, I think there has to be struggles along the way.

Through this experience, students can become more confident and prepared to face racial bias and minority issues in the outside adult world, although the following statements represent a positive outcome that is achieved in a negative manner.

The bottom line is that when you get into the real world you discover the things you deal with here you are going to deal with there. . . . When you come out of here you are not weak, you are stronger.

If you get through this, you are going to be all right.

It makes you a stronger person, and that is a key positive thing because in the real world, let's face it, you will be facing racism whether you like it or not.

I never used to really question the system. I would say it was me. I have the problem, but it's not me, it's the system, and I'm not afraid now.

I'd say the one good thing that happened to me was coming to this institution. Not only did I grow up getting to know myself and getting to know who I was as a Chicano, but coming from New Mexico where everyone was pretty much Chicano, to California where I am this Latino who is more than just a Mexican man coming over here and fitting in and figuring out exactly where I fit in as a Chicano, not just a Latino from California. Coming in from the top of my class in a public school into a small private institution where all these White students, being from private high schools just like the college. I realized that I wasn't at the same level. As one Latino told me, who was an upper classman, you may start off behind but in two years you will be caught up. In two years, I was caught up and I'm right up there, in fact past some of them. At the same time, you realize that you did get an education and you reflect on that and you ask yourself, how can I help Latin Americans in the future that come from other school systems? I think we ought to find ways to let them know exactly where they're at, and that even though you are behind, its just that you haven't had the same education, but by going to the same college you will have that education and you will catch up.

I think I came to college hoping to learn a lot more about myself and find my original identity, so I would say to all these people, do that before you come here because there's not going to be a lot of people you can identify with.

Students provided sound advice to their peers regarding how best to deal with academics. Asking for help was one element they believed incoming students needed to know to assist them in their scholarly pursuits.

One example is to get a mentor, whether it's a professor or an upperclassman. Students need to have somebody who can help them throughout college to make sure their first year is as enjoyable and pleasant as possible.

Students, like other Americans, are saturated with media portrayals of minorities. Too often they are portrayed as violent, negligent, disrespectful individuals who are lacking in morals and intelligence. For example, students commented,

Our mutual racial biases block the possibility to find a two-way road in solving these problems. It is much more convenient and easy to stay within your comfort zone, within your world of set views, beliefs, and values. We as human beings are sometimes so rigid in our beliefs and judgments.

My roommate already had some preconceived notion that I was a giant basketball player, or terrorist who might assault him in his sleep; funny, we have the same preconceived notions about them.

People just automatically put a label on you and you are stuck with it and it's hard. People don't take the time to get to know people before they say this and that about them.

It's just something you learn, like there are a lot of people who feel that the Islamic Club is a militant club, even though we are a bunch of nice people who are just trying to live our lives. We are a small minority on this campus. I can count all of us on all of my fingers, but they think we are terrorists and things like that.

They [White students] don't have any idea of what Latinos are . . . just that those are the people who are trying to come in and take our jobs.

Ignorance and an unwillingness to overcome biases and prejudice were sighted as injurious to the campus community, as the following students describe.

It was the first time I felt as though people didn't actually want to touch my hand. It made me feel like I was less of a person.

Everybody was referring to the African people as savages, and that just blew me out, and I couldn't understand what was going on. I said that first of all we need to stop talking about the African people as savages, and this girl got upset and asked, What is the politically correct term to call them?

I was put down a lot by these White people and I never realized they were putting me down until I came here and people asked me if I was nuts. . . .

It's just really sad when people say that I'm not a real American because I don't have American values.

One student mentions a White student's ordeal regarding cultural differences.

He assumes that he cannot talk about Black issues, because he's White and because he's assuming that the Black student will assume he really has nothing to contribute, that makes him uncomfortable.

Another student suggests,

> Sometimes I think that finding something in common other than race is probably one of the best ways to improve relations.

Two powerful statements made by students in the interview transcripts addressed problems, but also offered possible solutions. The first statement referred to the students' lack of critical reflection.

> I think that there are often times we don't critically reflect, and I think that's a downfall for a lot of students here. We don't put ourselves in the other person's shoes so we just assume that because we come from this environment. But if we're supposed to be intellectuals, we are supposed to be able to get beyond that. It's about critically reflecting to find out why it's just not one way.

A second statement discusses the concept of "the bubble," a protective encapsulation for students not desiring to look at cultural differences.

> I think the important thing is not staying in that bubble, getting involved in different organizations. That's the only way you're going to learn about them, you can't sit around and say all White people are like this and all White people are like that. What I don't see enough of is White students coming into organizations, and I think that's a problem. They expect to learn everything in a class in an hour about students of color and that is impossible.

Summary

Fitting into a particular group has been a difficult task for minority students. Consequently, several factors seem to influence the educational gains that students of color receive from their college experiences, such as student characteristics, college environments, efforts toward involvement, and racial status. Students who enroll in smaller colleges appear to be more involved in campus activities, often attributable to the "human scale" environment. From the students' voices throughout this study, it clearly is very difficult for students of color to be anonymous in their settings due to their relatively small numbers, which also affect opportunities for leadership and involvement in activities related to race or culture. These can become overwhelming and burdensome.

Therefore, this study may be in sharp contrast to the previous involvement studies that report the more involved students are the most likely they are to persist through to graduation. Perhaps becoming too involved in racial-type activities due to one's feeling of responsibility is an area that needs to be explored in the literature as a caveat for involvement. In classroom environments, the "only one" syndrome also may be a serious link to success for students of color and their ability to concentrate on academic work on the same cognitive plane as their White counterparts.

Student bodies are diverse in age, gender, culture, race, and ability. Therefore, we should try to understand students from a holistic perspective to help them maximize their learning experiences. How often do we really think about strategically planning our efforts to consider a student's background and its influence on his or her participation in the college experience? Are we proactive in our efforts to identify students who may need support to become successful graduates? Do we inform and identify those people who could and should get involved to support us in our efforts?

7

DISCUSSIONS, CONCLUSIONS, AND SUGGESTIONS

Discussions

This research investigation addressed three questions: (1) How do minority undergraduates experience learning outside the classroom? How do they characterize such experiences? (2) How does racial identity influence minority students' learning experiences outside the classroom? (3) How does campus climate influence minorities' out-of-classroom learning? To uncover these responses, we asked additional questions: What campus-based initiatives were in place to assist multicultural students in their transition to the collegiate environment? What services did the university provide to address the unique social and cultural needs of multicultural students? Did the university acknowledge and promote multiculturalism and diversity among its student population through special programming initiatives?

The first question regarding the minority undergraduate learning experience outside of the classroom was addressed in a number of the comments provided across category data. Students' experiences varied with regard to positive and negative encounters in the academic setting. Many who reported positive experiences can be characterized as having involvement in various programming initiatives and school leadership positions.

Additional positive experiences that students identified outside of the classroom environment included the relationships many established with administrators and faculty members. The importance of establishing relationships with individuals on the collegiate campus is important for all students, but this issue becomes a matter of utmost importance for the minority student. The importance of these relationships is attributed to many of the issues discussed in the previous sections stemming from incongruity between individual and institutional cultural patterns and norms.

Some of the negative out-of-classroom experiences advanced by the respondents included the institution's lack of commitment to promoting diversity and multiculturalism. A natural outpouring of this lack of initiative on the institution's part has resulted in communities that have become stagnant and uninterested in meeting the needs of a diverse student population. Comments provided in several of the categories speak to the seeming lack of interest and respect for minority student culture.

In addressing this question, institutions should not only strive to meet the academic needs of their student populations, but also focus on meeting the social and psychosocial needs of these individuals. Especially for the minority student, out-of-classroom engagements, primarily social in nature, constitute perhaps the most important component in their collegiate experience. According to Hughes (1987), socially oriented climates are crucial for learning and growth for many minority students on majority campuses—climates that are often diametrically opposed to the existing institutional environment.

The second question involving minority student identity and its subsequent effect on student learning was addressed in several categories cited in the conceptually clustered matrix. The category, "Ask anyone—they'll tell you . . . ," highlighted the students' dismay at being "required" to serve as designated spokespeople for their race. Additionally, the students' identity development was intimately tied to what one author termed "the double consciousness" mentality that the minority student often adopts in culturally different settings. Minority students, while negotiating their development as college students, must simultaneously negotiate their development as individuals of color. Institutions must be cognizant of the minority students' two-pronged progression through the various development and identity stages.

Literature focusing on college student development in general, and minority college student development in particular, provides an important theoretical framework which each institution could use to guide their practice. Evans, Forney, and Guido-DiBrito (1998) posit,

> Because student development theories focus on intellectual growth as well as affective and behavioral changes during the college years, they also encourage the collaborative efforts of student services professionals and faculty in enhancing student learning and maximizing positive student outcomes in higher education settings. (p. 5)

The parochial view of the collegiate experience held by the academic and student affairs professional must be expanded to include a more holistic approach to meeting student needs, especially those of the minority student. As the previous quote asserts, a collaborative effort in bridging best practices in student learning and development theory, with cognitive development theory and pedagogical protocol, can only serve to enhance student learning, growth, and development—the raison d'être of academe.

Finally, in looking at the influence of campus climate on student learning, numerous respondents provided valuable insight on their experiences. According to Edgert (1994), a "better understanding of campus climate may be a critical element in enhancing diversity in our colleges and universities" (p. 51). Many of the students spoke about the need of adjusting what appeared to be on many campuses a "chilly climate." A lack of interest in diversity, a lack of support for multicultural student populations, and a lack of opportunities provided to minority campus constituents were a few of the reasons identified to support these claims.

Edgert (1994) additionally reports, "Of particular interest is the relationship between perceptions of campus climate and student behavior . . . " (p. 61). A true adherence to student development theory informs us of the impact of the environment on the person and the requisite outcome on student behavior. For the minority student, the person and environment mix can be so incongruous that the overall educational experience evokes displeasure with the setting academic. Several comments provided by the respondents support this assertion, comments regarding the indifferent and sometimes hostile environments in which they matriculate.

Institutions must be conscious of the out-of-classroom environment the minority student negotiates as a day-to-day experience. The environment should provide sufficient challenge for the student, but opportunities and support must be additional pieces included in this puzzle. Many minority students view these higher educational settings with a "jaundiced eye." Their experiences are colored by cutthroat competition, social isolation, and a lack of respect for their cultural norms and behaviors (Fleming, 1984).

The questions framing this study served as a template upon which the research investigation was developed. In addition to serving as guiding constructs to probe into the minority students' undergraduate experience, these questions served to highlight a number of competing interests as they related to these students' matriculation. Although this study focused on a select number of liberal arts institutions, the concerns, issues, and problems these students encountered are found in many other higher educational contexts. This speaks to the importance of the collaborative relationships the institutions must cultivate with their respective minority student population.

Conclusions

There are several final points we would like to make. First, research data are good examples of what might be learned about institutions and their students by asking them to share their opinions. Some opinions are certainly biased, but still represent the students' frame of reference, which gives us as student affairs professionals and faculty some valuable, basic information.

Second, this research illustrates how events can go astray at institutions when the students and/or public becomes confused about the mission and values of that college. The institution must be consistent in its message if it wants anyone to truly believe in an abstract statement regarding its values and motives for existence.

Third, these transcripts have illustrated just how complex the issue of race and ethnicity can be in higher education. It shows that considering the issues among Whites versus Blacks or the majority versus the minority is not enough. As professionals and faculty, we must be cognizant of the fact that there are racial tensions and confusions about and among all races and nationalities, and we should be ready to lead all students in their efforts to sort through these and other developmental issues.

Finally, we have learned much regarding the value of qualitative research, along with some of its limitations. It does offer a texture and life to the research that helps clarify many concepts and issues. In this case, it created a greater sense of understanding for us with regard to minority students and how they view the world.

No claims are made about appropriate practices or policies of the institutions in this study or how institutions choose to conduct their campuses. No claims are made about a right or wrong way to assist students in their learning given the fact that a simple development theory does not or should not diagnose all students the same way all the time. No claims are made to which one may assume that the voices of these students should represent or speak for any or all students of color. Even though many of the students have chosen to reveal their frustration about their educational experiences, we are clearly aware that there are students of color who have many different experiences, more positive and more negative, with their peers, institutional agents, and college environment.

Yet, given current rates of retention, graduation rates, and adjustment problems for students of color that continue to plague the literature on minority students' experiences, one should at least pause and reflect on their words in this study. We as professionals should at least think about our current practices. Even in the midst of great efforts to support students of color, we need to critically reflect on how to make life more bearable, to think about students' backgrounds prior to enrollment, and to add structures and creative ways to make sure that we "hear" their concerns.

Suggestions and Thoughts

At the close of the day, most students really want to be a part of campus life. Most just want to know that they can participate and that their participation will be recognized and appreciated. Therefore, campuses might think to incorporate recognition programs during the year and give small tokens of appreciation to those students who go beyond the call of duty to make the campus an environment that is welcoming for all.

In our profession of student affairs and higher education, we are stuck on the belief that people should be changed by our programming efforts—almost to the point of converting everyone from a unique point of view to one of universal acceptance according to student affairs. Therefore, we have become narrow in our own practices and beliefs to truly embrace differences that are beyond the notions of what we would consider as fair and just. As educators, we should ensure that every voice is heard in order to bring about a greater understanding of students' experiences, beliefs, and values. Campuses need to hold forums around controversial topics to help students think critically about them. Facts, feelings, and beliefs should be shared and the forums should be led and guided by those who can develop and maintain a safe environment. One rule might be that all are free to express themselves in any terms, with any word as long as they are respectful and give reasons for their actions.

Incorporating these students' comments into the day-to-day operations and using them to reflect upon how the institution conducts business is very important. Multicultural students' perspectives need to be included in the marketing, recruitment strategies, retention plans, and curriculum of the institution. In addition, institutional agents need to consider all diverse groups, not just those students who exhibit so-called acceptable behavior. Sometimes those students who appear most different would bring a refreshing voice to the work of professionals and educators in higher education.

Let us revisit the definition of a university—a liberal education. What should the university or college experience do for students? In considering the voices of students represented in this book, we as student affairs educators begin our quests to challenge and support these students throughout their college experiences. The question therefore is, "Do we not know how to develop multicultural students or do we not care about their development?" After years of programming, workshops, classes, and other interventions surrounding diversity and multiculturalism, we seem to have made little gains in getting our students, peers, and faculty to critically address differences that exist among groups. Stated another way, we have not found the voice through our similarities that would allow us to discuss our differences in a sincere and intellectual way.

What we seem to have created through our efforts toward multicultural initiatives has been a climate of political correctness, where students and other institutional agents are afraid to discuss the "ism," especially in issues of race, culture, and ethnicity. It is obvious that students' educational experiences both in and out of class are affected by this awkward and oppressive situation. Students are afraid to discuss racial issues, so many remain ignorant by holding preconceived notions and stereotypes. For example, Levine and Cureton (1998) capture the same essence in their study of students' attitudes and perceptions about multiculturalism: "Multiculturalism is a painful subject on campus today. Students don't want to discuss it. In group interviews, students were more willing to tell us intimate details of their sex lives than to discuss race relations on campus. . . . In fact, when focus groups were asked about the state of race relations at their colleges the usual response was silence" (p. 72).

Students of color continue to perceive the college campus and environment totally different than White students. Issues of alienation, isolation, and tokenism become important factors when one considers their weight on the academic and social success and educational outcomes for students of color. Those factors are rarely considered when retention rates, probation rates, or graduation rates are presented.

As agents of our institutions, we might need to make sure that all constituencies know that a diverse student population adds value to everyone's educational experiences; however, minority students do not easily accept this notion. For example, students of color complained about being continually asked to educate Whites about minority issues. Other students say that they did not come to college to educate Whites. This theme is repeated in Levine and Cureton's (1998) study as well.

Therefore, we must encourage White students to share some of their experiences about various issues. We must make sure that we encourage all students to claim a true American (United States) heritage that includes the history of all groups of people who have influenced our culture and society. We are at the point in student affairs and higher education where our effort has taught us what not to say, that is, to be politically correct; however, we are left without a language or communication technique that would teach us what to say. Therefore, we need to be comfortable with the notion that we are going to offend someone, sometime, somewhere, about something. Get use to it. Be prepared to say you are sorry and give a rationale for your assumption. Apologize and ask for information and a language that would be acceptable to use. For example, how would one know if a woman wants to be called African American or Black, or if a man wants to be called Hispanic or Chicano, or White or European American, without the person giving some kind of information about his or her preference. We are not going to have all the answers in every situation, yet we should not fail to constantly strive to learn about cultural issues.

We have also grown deaf to multiculturalism and diversity training. Some professionals believe that because they have been to a multicultural training workshop, they are not prejudiced and have all the information needed to be successful with multicultural students. We have become slack when it comes to making an effort to be inclusive. We are constantly moving toward a campus that is exclusive and self-segregating, rather than inclusive. For a university or college, segregation does not lend itself to a quality liberal education or produce well-developed, civilized people who should know history, culture, and problem solving in order to take an active role in society.

From this study and similar studies, clearly multiculturalism remains to be one of the most unresolved issues across college campuses today. In fact, surveying the global landscape, multiculturalism will continue to be one of the most challenging issues that any leader will have to face.

The following are questions for all student affairs professionals and educators to consider:

- Do we really know enough about all students to effectively serve them in sufficient ways?

- Have we considered what students know about the world and have we incorporated that knowledge into our repertoire of skills and information to serve them?

- Have we fully used the resources that are available through technology to learn about students, their community, and the world? In other words, are we taking advantage of the tools we have to make us informed professionals?

- Why don't we as student affairs professionals feel compelled to learn and know about all Americans or at least know enough about the issues of multicultural students to point them to the most appropriate resources?

- How many times a year do we put ourselves in a totally different cultural context to understand our students' communities of origin?

If we are going to work within a college or school environment, we must equip ourselves with the skill base to interact, teach, serve, and counsel students from a global and contextual perspective that takes into account their culture. If we say we are student affairs professionals and educators, we must know how to assist any student from any background. If we do not know how to assist a student, we should act in good faith to make sure that he or she gets to the person who will know. To the surprise of many professionals, is it not always the multicultural center on campus, because we are all responsible for all students.

Professionals must be committed to the following actions:

- Relate continuing education to the multicultural students and the cultural differences that are present among White students.
- Address facts versus assumptions pertaining to students of color. Many times professionals do not have a clue about realistic facts concerning issues with students of color.
- Recognize that most policies and procedures were not developed with multicultural students in mind.
- Remain committed to quality and excellence through high expectations and support.
- Be the initiator of greetings. Saying hello and asking a multicultural student's name makes this person feel less isolated and gives him or her some contact with a professional on campus. Although others might be sincere in their efforts to serve students of color, they must quickly find other reasons to form a friendship or affiliation with them, otherwise the multicultural students will feel chosen only because of status.
- Be committed to seeing the world and the college experiences through the eyes of students.

As professionals, we must acknowledge the following facts.

- History as we have been taught is not totally correct, and we must find, learn, and tell the truth when it comes to the United States and the development of this country. Racism and prejudice against groups of people continue to be a real issue.

- Many programs and services are developed without the consideration of multicultural students' experiences and background.

- If we develop financial aid packages, recruitment materials, and other initiatives to attract students of color, we should make sure that we give them the courtesy of acknowledging them once they have enrolled.

- Professionals could become competent in their management and administrative ability to deal with differences and to resolve conflict and teach students how to do the same.

- Professionals might join organizations that may bring a different perspective about students of color than traditional professional organizations.

Organizations and institutions could consider the following actions:

- Make sure the institution represents itself to students realistically regarding diversity. For an institution to succeed, it must find ways to maximize the contribution of all its agents and students. Some institutions are filled with barriers that prevent people from contributing all their skills, ideas, and energies to the institution's success. Expressed in conscious and unconscious behaviors as well as routine practices, procedures, and bylaws, these barriers are often rooted in the very culture of an institution. Typically, they favor people who look and act like the leaders of the institution. To those they favor, the barrier is invisible; but to those who confront them daily, these barriers can be demeaning, discouraging, and insurmountable.

- Do not allow emotions to run high regarding organizational policy and planning. Give students, faculty, and administrators materials that they can read and think about once they leave versus a feeling of old-time revival services.

- Keep the focus on facts and education.

- Provide opportunities for professionals and educators to be engaged in multicultural contextual settings in order to learn and build one's knowledge base about students. In addition, organizations might consider a reward and merit system to encourage one to become more engaged in learning about students of color. Before an institution can expect to gain the full commitment and contributions of all its agents and students, exclusive barriers must be recognized and removed. Removing the barriers cannot be accomplished by a multicultural awareness workshop, an ethnic foods week, or a valuing diversity initiative. Building an inclusive institutional culture requires a serious commitment to fundamental changes in the structures, behaviors, expectations, operating procedures, human resources systems, formal and informal reward systems, leadership practices, competency requirements, and culture of the organization.

Magolda (1993) uses feminist perspectives to make this last point explicit. For example, feminist theorists "believe that behavior is developed through interactions with others in particular contexts. Moreover, the concept recognizes that gender-related behavior is fluid; it changes depending on context and other factors that interact with gender-related behaviors, such as race, class, or ethnicity. This conceptualization leads to a view of gender differences as context-based rather than as enduring, universal entities" (as cited by Deaux and Major, 1990; Thorne, 1990, p. 16).

In support of feminist contextual perspectives, we must move forward in racial and ethnic research by critically evaluating existing concepts and creating new epistemologies to ground conceptual framework and theories while providing sound methodological application. Multiculturalism models cannot be subsumed under a single model. Unfortunately, many multicultural models are under attack for their divisiveness (D'Souza, 1991; Fuchs, 1990; Wiley, 1993). Multiculturalism is not embodied in a single model; it is a response to increases in the number of minority populations, and it is concerned primarily with issues of educational opportunity and equality to improve knowledge. Traditional methods often do not afford the opportunity to use self, history, and current context to address issues of diversity. Relying too heavily on these traditional or single multicultural approaches can only limit the effectiveness of strategies designed to facilitate an effective campus-wide multicultural initiative (Banks, 1989; Stage and Manning, 1992; Stage and Hamrick, 1994).

The first significant issue that affects the climate on a college campus is the barrier of language and communication, which is personal and unique depending on one's background and experiences. This barrier is imposed in the academic arena when faculty do not recognize the various communication styles of students (Watson, 1996). Zane (1991) indicates that students of color and international students have the greatest anxiety and stress levels among college students directly related to their struggle to reconcile home cultures with the college campus. Home culture includes the language and communication style of the students with their respective families, community members, peers, and so forth, often misunderstood within institutions of higher education.

As educators, we might increase the one-on-one interactions we maintain with students to understand their needs as individuals. This kind of interaction would also give educators some indication of how to design programs and services to assist students. If language and communication are misunderstood, some students will become alienated from the mainstream or choose to isolate themselves, only socializing with others who share similar values and communication styles. More important, poor academic performance may result if professors do not recognize and accept these diverse communication styles.

The second issue that affects campus climate concerns acts of intolerance. Schmidt (1992) states that it is one thing to be offended by speech and another altogether to be directly threatened by words accompanied by menacing behavior. The controversy facing institutions of higher education at this time seems to reflect the disagreement between freedom of speech, even when the speech hurts, and the effects of hurtful speech which markedly results in acts of intolerance against ethnic and minority groups.

As majority and nonmajority students begin to articulate society's discussions of equality and fairness, institutions of higher education must prepare themselves to deal with such differences. As we consider issues of multiculturalism, we must learn not to make the issue one of emotional outrage. We must learn to discuss our individual experiences in a manner that other people can relate to and perhaps develop empathy in their understanding of our diverse experiences.

The third issue affecting campus climate is the dissension surrounding multicultural educational programming. A representative from the Commission on Civil Rights (1990) states that institutions are not interested in training faculty and students in dispute resolution or sensitivity. It has been consistently argued that colleges and universities have an obligation to respond to a more diverse society and to contribute to a more coherent view of knowledge and life for both the personal and social development of their students (Katz, 1989). The longer institutions of higher education avoid addressing diversity issues, the wider the gap will become between White students and students of color, faculty and students, and administrators and students.

As educators begin to define a quality education, the ideas, culture, and history of all races must be considered. Katz (1989) reports that institutions can no longer teach from a monocultural perspective. Norms and values must now be challenged in the classroom, workplace, and home; homogeneity is not, nor has it ever been, educationally sound. Boyer (1987) argues that "the undergraduate experiences must prepare students to see beyond the boundaries of their own narrow interests and discover connections that are global" (p. 232).

Appendixes

Appendix A
GENERAL ASSURANCES

GENERAL ASSURANCES AND PROCEDURES

Data will be collected from the institutions according to review procedures of each institution and only aggregated information will be reported. All findings will be reviewed by the institution before any formal publication is undertaken. No school will be identified with respect to any survey data or any findings resulting from this project.

A. **Subjects.** College students of African American, Hispanic, Native American, and Asian [American] descent will be invited to participate in this project. The professional staff serving as the campus contact will select these students. No student participant should be under the age of 18 [years of age].

B. **Activities.** Students will be interviewed about their extracurricular [or co-curricular] life at their particular college. The research investigators will conduct these interviews.

C. **Risks.** Interviews will be conducted in a group format. Students will be informed that all of their viewpoints are valued and that no one is to challenge another student's point of view.

D. **Protection of Subjects' Rights and Welfare.** Should any students be sensitive about talking about their feelings or about any other aspect of these activities, they may withdraw from the project at any time as stipulated in the consent form. Data obtained from the schools will be reported only in the aggregate. Neither schools nor students will be identified [in this study].

E. **Benefits.** Although no direct or immediate benefits may accrue to participants, the overall benefit is that our study will enable us to identify factors that promote campus environments associated with increased retention and success of [multicultural students] in majority [sic] White colleges.

F. **Voluntary Participation.** Students will complete a consent form before participating in the study. This form will include pertinent information regarding the study and its related activities.

Appendix B
CONSENT FORM

CONSENT FORM

You have been asked to participate in a study concerning students' learning experiences outside of the classroom. If you choose to participate, you will be asked to become involved with a one- to two-hour group meeting with six to ten other students from your college. In addition, you will be asked to complete a short survey dealing with your impressions of yourself and to fill out a short demographic sheet. It will take about two hours to participate in the small-group meeting and to complete the survey.

There are no foreseeable risks or discomforts associated with this study other than what is normally associated with telling someone you do not know about your typical college activities. Answering questions about your college life is not likely to cause any major discomfort or unpleasantness. The benefit you may gain from this study is minimal, although the knowledge gained from this study may contribute to a better understanding of students' learning experiences.

The data from this study will be summarized and reported as group data. Information that is gathered about you will not be reported to anyone in a manner that would identify you personally. If the data are presented at a conference or if they are reported in an article leading to publication in a journal or book, your personal responses will not be identified. You may withdraw from this study at any time. Your continued enrollment in your school or college will not be affected by your decision to not participate. A summary of the results will be made available to you upon completion of the study.

If you have any questions concerning any aspect of this project, you may contact [the coinvestigators at their respective e-mail and mailing addresses. Full addresses are noted here.] Thank you for your willingness to participate in this study.

[signed, coinvestigators]

Your signature below indicates you have read the above material and agree to participate in this study. Your signature also indicates you consent to being taped during the small-group interview.

Signature	Date
Printed Name	Date

Appendix C
DEMOGRAPHIC FORM

DEMOGRAPHIC INFORMATION

School _____ Date _____

Class: Freshman   Sophomore   Junior   Senior

Major _____

Ethnicity _____

Country of origin if not United States_____

Did your parents attend college? _____ Yes _____ No

Appendix D
FACILITATOR FORM

ADVICE TO FACILITATORS

1. Be sure to review the information in your letter of [Date], accompanying these instructions. [letter of invitation]
2. Ask students to read and sign the consent form. Collect forms from participants before beginning the interview or completing any demographic information.
3. Ask participants to complete the demographic information sheet and the Racial Identity Scale.
4. Explain the exact nature of the study briefly. Then provide the short introduction (in your own words) at the top of the page. Assure them that they will not be quoted as individuals.
5. Remember to help the person coding the tapes by commenting on visual cues. For example, when students indicate their positions (rating from 1 to 4), in question 1, state that there are four persons responding to the question, and that three respondents state their answer as 2 and one respondent answers with a rating of 3.
6. If the discussion covers the information elicited in future questions, please skip those questions.
7. If someone looks as if they want to contribute [a comment], encourage him or her to do so.
8. If someone becomes emotional, acknowledge the difficulty involved in responding. Continue with your interview if possible. Be sure to speak privately with the distressed student during the debriefing time following the completion of the interview. *Do not leave that student unattended.*
9. If one person tries to monopolize the discussion, ask others to respond to his or her ideas. Direct the discussion to other members to bring them into the conversation. Use verbal and nonverbal ways to achieve this task.
10. Adopt an open mind. Try to set aside your own values, background, and experiences as you facilitate this discussion of the participants.

Thank you for your cooperation!

Appendix E
INTERVIEW PROTOCOL

INTERVIEW PROTOCOL

[Interviewer reads this script before turning on tape recorder, signing consent forms, or beginning the actual interview.]

"Thank you very much for participating in this group discussion about your experiences at _____ [name of college]. We are interested in hearing your perceptions of what life is like for you here at _____ [college]; in short, your story. Also, we are interested in learning about specific ways that [your college] has been responsive to your needs. You, as individuals, will not be quoted in our report. However, your ideas will be summarized and generalized."

1. Please indicate your level of contentment here [on college campus] on a scale of 1 to 4 with 4 being very contented and 1 being unsettled. (Ask for a show of hands.) Explain your rating.
2. Please describe the single most positive experience you have had here.
3. In what specific ways does the institution demonstrate an appreciation of your racial/ethnic background? Faculty? Other students?
4. What are the pros and cons about this institution that you would present to minority students [who are] thinking of coming here [to this campus]?
5. What advice would you give to minority students who have decided to come here, in terms of how to cope effectively?
6. What fears, if any, do you have about being successful or not being successful academically here?
7. What is the one thing that you would take from here that would improve life for minority students on other campuses?

Optional questions (or for use in doing follow-up probe questions).

8. When you get upset, where do you go for support?
9. Please describe the single most negative experience you have had here.
10. How has your involvement on campus affected your feelings about the institution (e.g., on-campus living, social events, campus employment, student government, and/or leadership activities)?
11. What hopes, fears, or expectations did you have when you entered? Have they changed? How?
12. Do you expect to graduate from here? If not, why?

Appendix F
CONTENT AREAS

Use small-group interview format. Content theme areas for probing are

- Perceptions of the campus and its mission
- Campus culture
- Impressions about the student body in general
- Impressions about one's own peer group
- Feelings about self (self-esteem)
- Perceptions about self as a student of color (including racial identification)
- Learning environment within classroom
- Interactions between and among students (on campus)
- Interactions among group members (small-group interview)
- Relationship between interviewer and group members
- Future view of self
- Relationship with faculty and staff within/outside classroom

REFERENCES

Abraham, A., and W. Jacobs. 1990. *Black and white students' perceptions of their college campuses.* Atlanta: A Southern Regional Educational Board, 24.

Allen, W. 1986. *Gender and campus race differences in black student academic performance, racial attitudes and college satisfaction.* Atlanta: Southern Education Foundation.

Anastasi, A. 1985. Interpreting results from multiscore batteries. *Journal of Counseling and Development* 64(1): 84–86.

Banks, J. 1989. Integrating the curriculum with ethnic content: Approaches and guidelines. In James A. Banks and C. A. Banks (eds.), *Multicultural education: Issues and perspectives.* Boston: Allyn & Bacon.

Barr, D. J., and L. Strong. 1988. Embracing multiculturalism: The existing contradictions. *NASPA Journal* 26(2): 85–90.

Birnbaum, R. 1988. *How colleges work.* San Francisco: Jossey-Bass, 86, 88, 93–94.

Bourdieu, P. 1977. The cultural transmission of social inequality. *Harvard Educational Review* 47: 545–55.

Bourdieu, P., and J. C. Passeron. 1977. *Reproduction in education, society and culture: Sage studies in social and educational change.* Beverly Hills, Calif.: Sage Publications.

Boyer, E. L. 1990. *Scholarship reconsidered: Priorities for the professoriate.* San Francisco: Jossey-Bass, 17, 25, 47.

Boyer, E. 1987. *College: The undergraduate experience in America.* New York: Harper & Row.

Brubacher, J. S., and W. Rudy. 1968. *Higher education in transition: A history of American colleges and universities, 1636–1976.* New York: Harper & Row.

Cheatham, H. 1991. *Cultural pluralism on campus.* Alexandria, Va.: American College Personnel Association.

Creswell, J. W. 1998. *Qualitative inquiry and research design: Choosing among five traditions.* Thousand Oaks, Calif.: Sage Publications.

Cross, L. 1991. Public Opinion and the NCAA Proposal 42. *Journal of Negro Education* 60(2): 181–194.

Cross, W. E. 1978. Black family and black identity: A literature review. *Western Journal of Black Studies* 2(2): 111–124.

D'Andrea, M., and J. Daniels. 1995. Addressing the developmental needs of urban, African-American youth: A preventive intervention. *Journal of Multicultural Counseling and Development* 23(1).

D'Souza, D. 1991. *Illiberal education: The politics of race and sex on campus.* New York: Free Press.

Deaux, K., and B. Major. 1990. A social-psychological model of gender. In D. L. Rhode (ed.), *Theoretical perspectives on sexual difference.* New Haven, Conn.: Yale University Press.

Denzin, N. K. 1989. *Interpretive interactionism.* Newbury Park, Calif.: Sage Publications.

Denzin, N. K., and Y. S. Lincoln. 1994. *Handbook of qualitative research.* Thousand Oaks, Calif.: Sage Publications.

Dorsey, M., and A. Jackson. 1995. Afro-American students' perceptions of factors affecting academic performance at a predominately white school. *Western Journal of Black Studies* 19(13): 192.

Edgert, P. 1994. Assessing campus climate: Implications for diversity. *New Directions for Institutional Research* 81(Spring): 61.

Erickson, F. 1986. Cultural differences and science education. *Urban Review* 18(2).

Evans, N. J., D. S. Forney, and F. Guido-DiBrito. 1998. *Student development in college: Theory, research, and practice.*

Jossey-Bass Higher and Adult Education Series. San Francisco, Calif.: Jossey-Bass.

Fleming, J. 1984. *Blacks in college.* San Francisco: Jossey-Bass.

Fuchs, L. H. 1990. *The American kaleidoscope: Race, ethnicity, and the civic culture.* Hanover, Conn.: Wesleyan UP.

Gall, M. D., W. R. Borg, and J. P. Gall. 1996. *Educational research: An introduction,* 6th ed. Reading, Mass.: Addison-Wesley Publishing Co.

Glaser, B. G., and A. L. Strauss. 1967. *The discovery of grounded theory.* Chicago: Aldine.

Glaser, K. 1978. Designing political institutions for multi-ethnic countries. Paper presented at annual meeting of the Third World Conference, Omaha, Nebraska.

Gordon, S. E., and C. B. Strode. 1992. Enhancing cultural diversity and building a climate of understanding: Becoming an effective change agent. In M. C. Terrell (ed.), *Diversity disunity and campus community.* National Association of Student Personnel Administrators Series. Washington, D.C.: NASPA.

Hopewood v. Texas, 78 F3d 932 1996.

Hughes, M. S. 1987. Black students' participation in higher education. *Journal of College Student Personnel* 28(6): 532–545.

Hurn, C. J. 1993. *The limits and possibilities of schooling: An introduction to the sociology of education.* Boston: Allyn and Bacon.

Ingle, 1994. *Charting campus progress in promoting ethnic diversity and cultural pluralism: Studying diversity in higher education.*

Ivey, A., M. Ivey, and L. Simek-Morgan. 1997. *Counseling and psychotherapy: A multicultural perspective,* 4th ed. Boston: Allyn & Bacon.

Jones, L. 2001. Creating an affirming culture to retain African-American students during the postaffirmative action era in higher education. In Lee Jones (ed.), *Retaining African Americans in higher education: Challenging paradigms for retaining students, faculty and administrators.* Sterling, Va.: Stylus Publishers.

Katz, J. 1989. The challenge of diversity. In C. Woolbright (ed.), *Valuing diversity.* Bloomington, Ind.: Association of College Unions-International.

Kuh, G. 1992. What do we do now? Implications for educators of How College Affects Students. *Review of Higher Education:* 352.

Kuh, G., J. Schuh, E. Whitt, R. Andreas, J. Lyons, C. Strange, L. Krehbiel, and K. Mackay. 1991. *Involving colleges: Successful approaches to fostering student learning and development outside the classroom.* San Francisco: Jossey-Bass.

Kuh, G., and R. E. Andreas. 1991. It's about time: Using qualitative methods in student life studies. *Journal of College Student Development* 32(5): 397–405.

Levine, A., and J. S. Cureton. 1998. *When hope and fear collide: A portrait of today's college student.* San Francisco: Jossey-Bass.

Lincoln, Y., and E. Guba. 1985. *Naturalistic inquiry.* Newbury Park, Calif.: Sage Publications.

Magolda, M. B. 1987. A rater-training program for assessing intellectual development on the Perry scheme. *Journal of College Student Personnel* 28(4): 356–364.

Magolda, M. B. 1992. *Knowing and reasoning in college: Gender-related patterns in students' intellectual development.* San Francisco: Jossey-Bass.

Magolda, M. B. 1993. The convergence of relational and interpersonal knowing in young adult's epistemological development. Paper presented at the annual meeting of the American Educational Research Association in April, Atlanta.

Miles, M. B., and A. M. Huberman. 1994. *Qualitative data analysis: An expanded sourcebook.* Thousand Oaks, Calif.: Sage Publications.

Moos, R. 1985. Psychosocial processes of remission in unipolar depression: Comparing depressed patients with matched community controls. *Journal of Consulting and Clinical Psychology* 53(3).

Nettles, M. T., A. R. Thoeny, and E. S. Gosman. 1986. Comparative and predictive analysis of Black and White students' college achievement and experiences. *Journal of Higher Education* 57(3): 289–318.

Newman, J. H. 1901. The idea of a university. In Charles W. Elliot (ed.), *The Harvard classics.* New York: P. F. Collier & Son, 60.

Parham, T. A., and J. E. Helms. 1981. The influence of black students' racial identity attitudes on preference for counselor's race. *Journal of Counseling Psychology* 28(3): 250–257.

Parham, T. A., and J. E. Helms. 1985. Attitudes of racial identity and self-esteem of black students: An exploratory investigation. *Journal of College Student Personnel* 26(2): 143–147.

Patton, M. Q. 1990. *Qualitative evaluation and research methods,* 2nd ed. Newbury Park, Calif.: Sage Publications, 10, 278, 285.

Paul, D. G. 1998. Bridging the cultural divide: Reflective dialogue about multicultural children's books. *New Advocate* 11(3): 241–251.

Polkinghorne, D. E. 1989. The use of natural language in counseling psychology research. Paper presented at the annual meeting of the American Psychological Association in August, New Orleans, La.

Pouncey, P. 1993. Reflections on black separatism at American colleges. *Journal of Blacks in Higher Education* 1(Fall): 57–59.

Roebuck, J. B., and K. S. Murty. 1993. *Historically black colleges and universities: Their place in American higher education.* Westport, Conn.: Praeger Publishers.

Rubin, H. J., and I. S. Rubin. 1995. *Qualitative interviewing: The art of hearing data.* Thousand Oaks, Calif.: Sage Publications, 127.

Schmidt, B. 1992. The university and freedom. *Educational Record.*

Stage, F., and F. Hamrick. 1994. Diversity issues: Fostering campuswide development of multiculturalism. *Journal of College Student Development* 35(5): 331–336.

Stage, F., and K. Manning. 1992. *Enhancing the multicultural campus environment: A cultural brokering approach.* New Directions for Student Affairs, no. 60. San Francisco: Jossey-Bass.

Strauss, A. L. 1987. *Qualitative analysis for social sciences.* Cambridge, England: Cambridge University Press.

Strauss, A. L., and J. Corbin. 1990. Grounded theory methodology: An overview. In N. K. Denzin and Y. S. Lincoln (eds.), *Handbook of qualitative research.* Thousand Oaks, Calif.: Sage Publications.

Strenski, I. 1993. Recapturing the values that promote civility on the campus. *The Chronicle of Higher Education,* June 21.

Strong, R. 1986. New strategies, new visions. *Educational Leadership* 44(2): 52–54.

Sue, D. W., and D. Sue. 1990. *Counseling the culturally different.* New York: John Wiley & Sons.

Thorne, B. 1990. Children and gender: Constructions of differences. In D. L. Rhode (ed.), *Theoretical perspectives on sexual difference.* New Haven, Conn.: Yale University Press.

Tierney, W. G. 1992. Cultural leadership and the search for campuses. *Black Collegian.*

Watson, L. W. 1996. A collaborative approach to student learning, planning and changing. *Educational Leadership and Policy Journal* 27: 3.

Watson, L. W. 1998. The college experience: A conceptual framework to consider for enhancing students' educational gains. In K. Freeman (ed.), *The African American cultural and heritage in higher education research and practice.* Westport, Conn.: Greenwood.

Watson, L. W., and G. D. Kuh. 1996. The influence of dominant race environments on student involvement, perceptions, and educational gains: A look at historically black and predominantly white liberal arts institutions. *Journal of College Student Development* 37(4): 415–425.

Whitt, E. J., and G. D. Kuh. 1991. Qualitative methods in a team approach to multiple-institution studies. *Review of Higher Education* 14(3): 317–338.

Wiley, T. 1993. Back from the past: Prospects and possibilities for multicultural education. *Journal of General Education.*

Zane, N., S. Sue, L. Hu, and J. Kuon. 1991. Asian-American assertion: A social learning analysis of culture difference. *Journal of Counseling Psychology* 38(1): 63–70.